A·S·H·E·S

A·S·H·E·S

TRUE TALES FROM CRICKET'S
GREATEST STARS

An imprint of HarperCollins*Publishers*

AN ANGUS & ROBERTSON BOOK

An Imprint of HarperCollinsPublishers

First published in the United Kingdom by
Angus & Robertson (UK) in 1991
An imprint of HarperCollins
First published in Australia by
Swan Publishing Pty Ltd

Angus & Robertson (UK)
77-85 Fulham Palace Road, London W6 8JB
United Kingdom

A catalogue record for the book is
available from the British Library
ISBN 0 207 17153 X

Printed in Great Britain by Hartnolls, Bodmin, Cornwall

Contents

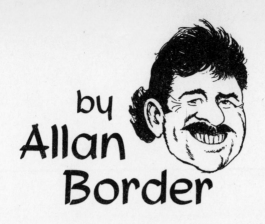

by
Allan
Border

AND THE BAND PLAYED ON

There is nothing like a live brass band to stir the musical soul. The Australians thought so, anyway, during our 1985 tour of England. We fell in love with the Hammond Sauce Works Band.

As names for musical ensembles went, we thought it was the catchiest since Sergeant Pepper's Lonely Hearts Club. There were 20 guys in this band and they all worked for the Hammond Sauce Works in Yorkshire. They performed each morning before play in the First Test at Headingley, and we thought they were great. Someone with an ear for music more finely-tuned than ours told us there were basic flaws in their technique, but that didn't matter a damn to this touring party. We loved them as much for their sense of humour as their virtuosity.

Our guys took great delight in shying cricket balls at them—making sure they fell well short, I assure you—as the Hammond Sauce Works boys did their stuff out there in the middle. Far from being intimidated, they enjoyed it immensely. It's hard to explain instant rapport between a visiting international cricket team and a local amateur brass band. But that's what it was. The Hammond Sauce Works Band was mentioned often—and with genuine affection—for the rest of the tour.

We arrived at Gloucester for a county match and were delighted to see what we thought were our Hammond Sauce Works mates out there making music. They *looked* like our mates and Wayne Phillips said: "Christ! Would you believe that? They're following us around the country. What a beauty!"

Wayne was wrong. We were all wrong. This was the Royal Military Band, no less. The top brass. They were here, we were told, in conjunction with the visit that day of Princess Di, patron of the Gloucestershire Cricket Club. Their presence brought back fond, recent memories of the Sauce Works lads and there was more than just a little nostalgia about the place as we warmed up for the start of play.

Australia won the toss, elected to bowl and we congregated on the balcony, listening to the closing stanzas of the Royal Military Band's final number. The cymbals were probably still vibrating from their very last clash when a voice boomed out over the ground's public address system:

"Ladies and gentlemen—would you please put your hands together for the. . . Hammond Sauce Works Band!"

I've never heard—or not heard—a hush like it. Complete silence, save for the raucous laughter of the Australian cricket team. Within seconds, the balcony was swarming with angry Gloucestershire officials demanding an explanation from our manager, Bob Merriman. Poor Bob didn't understand their problem at all, but when one of the officials—the club secretary, I think—started ranting and raving, our beloved leader started giving as good as he was getting.

In the midst of it all, Wayne Phillips emerged from the ground announcer's box, grinning hugely.

Yes, we all loved the Hammond Sauce Works Band— but Wayne was chairman of the fan club!

NOT THAT WAY, LADIES!

Jeff Thomson was known among his team mates as having one of the quickest wits in cricket. 'Thommo' was never lost for a word or a comeback and we saw him at his best—even if it was a bit naughty—at Leicester one morning during the 1985 Ashes tour.

Jeff was one of eight players warming up before the start of play with some sharp fielding practice in front of the members' pavilion. The exercise was being watched with interest by a group of spectators, some of them seeking autographs. It was fair-dinkum practice, with the ball being whacked by or deflected from the bat to the close fieldsmen. A few of the shots were getting through the cordon and sending the spectators scurrying.

A particularly sharp deflection slipped through 'Thommo's' fingers and struck a woman in the crowd a nasty blow in what commentators describe as "er . . . the groin". It floored her and the players jumped the fence to see if she was ok. It was quickly apparent that she was and as she was assisted to her feet, Jeff said: "If she wants to catch the ball, she shouldn't snatch at it."

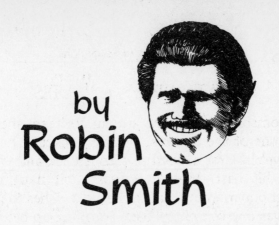

by
Robin Smith

MERV, MY XXXX MATE

Four-X was a word we all got very accustomed to hearing during my first Ashes experience.

It was the summer of 1989, the summer when an alien lifeforce known as Merv Hughes—allegedly a native of the planet Ocker—arrived in England and conquered all that stood in his way.

And it was the summer when he taught the inhabitants of his adopted country, Australia, how to speak the language of his fathers, the Ocker tongue, the language known as XXXX.

Evidence of the success of his mission to XXXX the world came early in the tour and it came in mysterious fashion. Suddenly, one bright summer morning, London was covered with a strange message from a faraway land.

On the side of the double-decker buses, in cinemas throughout the West End and, according to unconfirmed reports, outside public lavatories, Londoners were advised that "Australians couldn't give a XXXX for anything else".

Apart from what? They wondered.

It was clear that the message did not at first translate into recognisable English. But on closer inspection of the photographs above the words, it was possible to make out the faces of the Australian cricket team. Among them was the unmistakably intellectual visage of Marvellous Mervyn.

I didn't have long to wait for my first personal experience of the language of XXXX and to discover the true meaning of the word. It came at Headingley in the First Test.

Having been introduced to the man and his moustache by a series of short pitched balls, I soon realised that Merv was also an expert in that other extraterrestrial mind-craft known as 'winding the bastards up'.

It very soon became clear that his great strength was in using the language of XXXX to do just that, simply by using the XXXX word when you least expected it, as in "Good XXXX morning" or "G'XXXXday". He also had the ability to make "good XXXX" sound like an invitation to step outside. And quite often he did.

He was most helpful as well when it came to passing on technical tips about my batting like, "Mate, if you just turn the XXXX bat over, you'll see the XXXX instructions on the XXXX back".

And "Does yer XXXX husband play cricket as well?"

But, having ruled out the hook shot that did for me first time, I found that Merv and I were able to communicate much better. And I remember the occasion when we finally started to speak the same language.

It was just after I had played and missed at him, when he walked down the track to advise me to "XXXX off". The reason being, in his words, "You can't XXXX bat."

Next ball, a shortish one outside the off stump, hit the boundary rope before the stubble on his chin had

a chance to bristle. Ignoring the umpire's signal of four runs, I decided to make my ground at the bowler's end and offer a few words of my own.

"Hey Merv," I said, "we make a fine pair, don't we?"

"Why's that?" he asked, somewhat startled.

"Well, I can't XXXX bat and you can't XXXX bowl."

And that, as they say, was that. Now we get on like a house on fire. After the last Test at The Oval, Merv caught me out in the England dressing-room, held out his hand and said, "Put it there, mate". We swapped jerseys and caps, had a couple of drinks and had our first real chat of the summer.

You might say that now we're XXXX good mates.

C'MON AUSSIE C'MON

by
Richie Benaud

THOSE CURIOUSLY MAD AUSTRALIANS

One of the great things in my life was playing cricket against England. Playing cricket against West Indies, South Africa, Pakistan, India and New Zealand was marvellous too, but the Ashes didn't exist in those matches. A subtle difference, but a very real one for someone brought up on the 1936–37 battle in Australia between the teams captained by Don Bradman and 'Gubby' Allen.

The Ashes are the reason why, even if the two teams are not the strongest in the world at a given time, there is still enormous interest in the cricket and in the results. If, by chance, they happen to be the two best at the time, then there is, as well, tension, pathos and humour. Sometimes there is even illusion.

When we were so comprehensively beaten by England in 1956, there was a certain amount of gloom in the camp. We won brilliantly at Lord's and lost at Headingley and Old Trafford and the man, more than any other responsible for our problems, was Jim Laker. He was the best of all offspinners of my time, though Hughie Tayfield, a different type of spinner, was also very effective on hard pitches. At Old Trafford, when Jim took his 19 wickets, Tony Lock at the other end took only one, mainly because he was turning the ball

so far it was difficult to lay the bat on it.

Batting late on the last day I was, quite rightly, and amusingly, on the receiving end of a blast of frustration from Tony because I had been spending a little extra time in repairing the pitch. As the ball flashed past my ear into Godfrey Evans's left glove, floating down the pitch came the immortal words, "Pat that one down, you little bastard." Jim Laker's eyes twinkled a little at that; as well as being a fine bowler, Jim had a delightful, dry sense of humour, although he didn't need too much of that when he took those 19 wickets against us. We were the ones needing to smile through gritted teeth!

Two years later England came to Australia, full of confidence, and the early matches of the tour did nothing to dent that. Just prior to the First Test in Brisbane they beat an Australian XI in Sydney by 345 runs, with Tony Lock taking 6/29 from 16 overs, assisted slightly by bowling into Fred Trueman's footmarks at the M. A. Noble Stand end. Two days later I was a shock selection as captain of the Australian team and, at the team meeting the night before the Test, one of the firm plans was to keep Fred off the pitch. As it turned out Fred had lumbago, which these days would be called a stress fracture, and had to pull out on the morning of the match. We stayed with the plan though, because 'Lockie' was in the side and, when Brian Statham bowled the first ball of the Australian innings and, as he always did, moved straight off the pitch, Jim Burke ostentatiously walked down the pitch and tapped down his 'spike marks' in line with middle stump.

We were very vigilant on this throughout the match, the Englishmen substituting 'bloody impossible' for 'vigilant', but Jim Laker gave the perfect response. On the Monday I was batting and as I watched in a mixture of horror and awe, Jim walked the whole length of the pitch, straight down from middle stump to middle stump. As he reached me I had my mouth open and speech ready and it was going to be along the lines of, "Would you mind getting off our bloody pitch, you're not at The Oval now," when a sixth sense had me glance down at his feet. He was wearing rubber-soled shoes. As he caught my eye, he was also wearing just the faintest twitch at the corners of his mouth!

Wally Grout was keeping wicket for Australia in that match, having earlier taken over from Don Tallon in the Queensland side. 'Deafy', so nicknamed because of a reputed slight hearing affliction that never seemed to impair his ability to hear the faintest snick, played his last Test against England at Trent Bridge in 1953. It was my first Test against England and it was the scene of some magnificent medium-pace bowling from

Alec Bedser. In those days batsmen were allowed to appeal against the light. On the fourth day we were in heaps of trouble at 6/81 with Tallon next in, on a 'pair'. In the first innings Bedser had bowled him with one which pitched leg and hit off. Bedser was bowling again.

I was sitting alongside Lindsay Hassett when 'Deafy' stood up and Lindsay said, "Hang on a moment until I have a look". Having had a glance out of the dressing-room side window and considered the combination of appalling light plus Bedser he said, "It's black out there 'Deafy', give it a go".

He certainly did. He hit 15 from the first few balls he received and then was out to a brilliant running catch in the outfield by Reg Simpson trying to smash Roy Tattersall for six. He returned to the dressing-room, beaming. It had never entered his mind that Hassett hadn't been instructing him to go for glorious victory and was unable to understand why stony silence greeted his return, until he gave his interpretation of events. At this point the members in the Trent Bridge pavilion were astonished to hear gales of laughter from the dressing-room occupied by those curiously mad Australians, the last batsman of whom had just played, in the circumstances of an Ashes war, one of the more extraordinary innings they had ever seen in the land of Larwood and Voce!

There have been some quaint things happen in cricket in England and Australia, the two countries responsible for the creation of the Ashes battles. Not all of the humour, nor the oddities for that matter, have always involved Test players; sometimes those trying to ease themselves into the Test arena were the notables. Take E. J. Diver for example, the first man to play for the

Gentlemen of England and the Players.

He also played for Surrey as an amateur and Warwickshire as a professional before the turn of the century and was spoken of, early in his career, as a possible England player in future Ashes battles. What dark conspiracy do you imagine took place to have him make his debut for Warwickshire against Notts, return bowling figures of 30.3-14-58-6, thus ensuring his team won the match and then not be given a bowl in the next game against his old county, Surrey? Thereafter he played for Warwickshire on more than 100 occasions and never again took a first class wicket. Perhaps his captain knew something that day.

No more odd, I suppose, than Lord Sheffield's decree in a match in the south of England shortly before the turn of the century. In 1891 he had taken his team to Australia, lost two Tests to one in a thrilling Ashes series, and presented to the hosts the Shield which bears his name "for competition by the different colonies". Some years later, not as agile as of yore but just as enthusiastic, he was captaining his team in very damp conditions. He decided that the Lordly feet should not be wet. The groundsman was summoned to scythe a 20-yard circle of grass at third man/long on, from which His Lordship never ventured. If the ball came to him he fielded it, otherwise it was a matter of attention for the ordinary people.

Worries abound in Ashes cricket. The batsman who is having something of a bad trot, the bowler who can't quite pitch it right, the wicket-keeper who feels the ball is not hitting the gloves as he would wish. Then there are the followers of the game whose favourites are slightly out of form and there are those whose nearest and dearest are part of the team and no one is certain how things will turn out for them.

One of my favourite cricketers of all time is Graham McKenzie. 'Garth' was just a kid when I took him on his first overseas tour aged 20 and, by the time the tour was over, he had played in the Lord's Test and bowled out England with a magnificent 5/37 from 29 overs and shared, with Alan Davidson at Old Trafford, that famous 98–run last-wicket stand which gave us the chance to retain the Ashes, which we did later the same day.

We brought him back as we took him away from Perth, a marvellous young man and a fine cricketer, improving all the time. When we left Western Australia, though, there were some misgivings. We were departing by ship from Fremantle and the last call had gone out for all visitors to go ashore. Graham's Mum and Dad were there and there was a vast crowd to see us off. I was watching the scene, leaning on the rail, very relaxed, looking at the streamers being thrown from the wharf.

I was also alone. Mrs. McKenzie joined me and wondered if she might ask a great favour.

"Certainly, Mrs. McKenzie."

"I'm just worried about Graham being lonely on the tour," she said. "You will look after him, won't you?"

I looked over Mrs. McKenzie's shoulder to where her son was standing some 20 yards away. I knew it was her son because I could see his head and those very, very broad shoulders. I could see nothing else of him because he was surrounded, at a conservative estimate, by 47 nubile 19-year-olds, all of whom were trying to say goodbye to him.

I looked back at Mrs. McKenzie. "Don't you worry," I said. "Once he settles down I'm sure he'll be okay!"

by Graham McKenzie

FANATICAL FRANK'S FOLLY

Thirty years after my first exposure to international cricket the scene has altered somewhat. Then, one of the most enjoyable experiences for an international cricketer was the extended ship journey.

This provided players with the opportunity to truly get to know their team mates away from cricket grounds, hotels, and airport or coach terminals, places where most of a cricketer's life is spent.

My first international cricket tour was in 1961, the last time the Australian team went by ocean liner all the way to England. In 1964 the Australians travelled from Fremantle to Bombay by ship and then on to London by air. Ever since teams have done the full journey by plane.

As you can imagine, shipboard life was quite relaxed. We particularly appreciated the fancy dress night when, by tradition, the team dressed as Arabs.

Such a night allowed the players the chance to relax in the anonymity of disguise rather than be constrained by the dinner suits that were compulsory at evening meal time. The Arab costume was easy to arrange, as the only requirement was a supply of bed sheets and some boot polish for moustaches and beards.

On such a night we cricketers were the centrepiece

of the dining room as we were seated in a 'clearing' on the floor, together with wine flagons and sumptuous food, which had to be eaten by hand.

Now one of the team was Frank Misson, the young fair-haired New South Wales pace bowler, who had shown great feats of stamina during the previous Australian season against West Indies.

He was a fitness fanatic. Wherever Frank travelled he had dining-room staff totally aware of his special health food needs. Frank's first duty on arrival at any hotel was to investigate the kitchen and give instructions on the preparation of his breakfast.

As a result Frank was well looked after by the staff, always receiving his meals promptly on arrival in the dining-room while the rest of us waited for our orders to be fulfilled.

As well as a strict diet, Frank also stuck to a running programme. Training runs on board ships offer little variety and on this trip Frank had only one suitable deck, one that allowed him to cover about 400 metres per circuit.

Frank was an avid runner so he'd complete lap after lap of this course. When our boat reached the tropics Frank ran in the evenings, before sundown; the rest of us would be congregated by the pool bar by then.

As it happened, part of Frank's course took him right by the pool bar. Frank would be cheered as he passed on each lap, and gradually obstacles such as deck chairs, stools and tables would be furtively pushed into his way in an endeavour to impede his progress.

Frank wouldn't even give us the satisfaction of a sidelong glance as he tried to avoid more and more obstacles on each succeeding lap. He just kept churning out the laps, improving his hurdling and climbing techniques in the process.

He looked simply magnificent . . . unfortunately soon after he was admitted to the ship's hospital with a bronchial disorder! And . . . he was the only player on the tour of England to have trouble with shin-soreness!

SEA-SNICK

During the ship journey to England for the 1961 Ashes series we stopped over in Ceylon, now Sri Lanka, for a game of cricket against the locals. At that stage we had done no cricket practice on board.

That was to happen in the last two weeks of the journey. Then, it had been decided, there would be compulsory workouts, 7.30 a.m. for excercises and 5 p.m. for skills practice.

As it turned out, to cope with this programming, more than one player was known to reverse his normal sleeping pattern by staying up all night, going directly to 7.30 a.m. training, then sleeping the day away, arising just in time to appear at the 5 p.m. session!

The ship's crew had agreed to set up nets together with a coir mat for the pitch. Conventional pads, bats and balls were to be used.

But for the Ceylon game preparation had only been eight days at sea. The ship arrived in Colombo Harbour around 6 a.m. and left about midnight, allowing enough time for a one-day fixture.

The first ball I received was quite an experience, as after eight days at sea I did not have land legs and it felt as though the pitch was moving under my feet as I faced up to the bowler.

Fortunately this swaying enabled me to get an inside edge to a legspinner which went to fine leg for one. If I hadn't swayed elegantly to the off I reckon I would have snicked the ball straight to slip off the outside edge and made an inglorious duck in my first innings overseas!

SNOOKERED!

I was the youngest member of the 1961 team that toured England. Before we set out on the lengthy ship's journey I had only briefly met many of the other team members. But once on board they were all keen to help me and acquaint me with shipboard life, many of them having done it all before.

One of those to offer advice was Wally Grout, the great wicket-keeper from Queensland. Wally was apparently a keen snooker player and kindly offered to instruct me in the art of the game.

He was adamant that I would be a more than competent player by the time I reached England, maintaining that I needed only to devote a few free hours to the learning curve during the trip over.

It seemed a nice gesture from one of the older players to a new boy and I was very grateful. But after three days at sea Wally had still not directed me to the snooker room. I made some enquiries as to its whereabouts only to be confronted with chuckles and smiles and assurances that the room, and the game, would eventuate.

I resolved to be patient, but in the end decided to ask a crew member where the snooker table was.

"Unfortunately we have left behind the gyroscopic room that compensates for the ship's movement," I was told. The penny dropped! I didn't mention snooker again on the trip.

And I had to wait for the next trip, three years later, for an opportunity to use the same story on a new tourist, Ian Redpath.

C'MON AUSSIE C'MON

by
Frank
Tyson

A MATTER OF NOBILITY

The English take their cricket very seriously, particularly when it concerns Test matches against Australia. I remember seeing a prewar—World War II, not World War I—black-and-white comedy film, *The Lady Vanishes*. In it the two comedians, Basil Radford and Naunton Wayne, arrive at London's Victoria Station on the boat train from Dover to find newspaper posters proclaiming in alarming headlines: "England Collapses" and "England Faces Disaster". Had the country suffered a major military defeat? No. It was the equally-serious crisis of the England cricket team finding itself on the verge of defeat against Bradman's 1938 side.

The whole cricketing world is well-acquainted with the legend of the Ashes and the deadly rivalry engendered by a Test series between England and Australia. Cricketers of every nationality—even those not directly involved—take sides. When I was a member of the England team which defeated Australia 3-1 in Australia in 1954-55, one conveniently partisan calypsonian from Trinidad sent me a record which, when played, proclaimed:

"We beat them quite easily,
Good captaincy by Len Hutton,
But the honours must go to 'Typhoon' Tyson."

28

We indeed! I wonder if that Caribbean gentleman has called any England side *we* since his countrymen began systematically 'blackwashing' the Poms in the 1980s!

Most people familiar with the Ashes story know of the famous obituary on English cricket published in the London *Sporting Times* in August, 1882. It bemoaned England's first defeat at the hands of William Lloyd Murdoch's Cornstalks and recorded its death, cremation and the subsequent transportation of its Ashes to Australia. The now traditional Test struggle for those Ashes began in Adelaide in the following winter, when the captain of the England touring side, the Hon. Ivo Bligh, proclaimed his crusade to regain the symbolic trophy.

But I wonder how many cricket enthusiasts know

how the physical Ashes and their Urn came into existence?

Originally it was thought that Miss Florence Murphy, an Australian lady from Beechworth, a shipboard companion of the England touring team, a governess in the employ of Australian squatocrat Sir William Clarke, the wife-to-be of Ivo Bligh and the future Countess of Darnley, was responsible. She was said to have persuaded some ladies of her acquaintance to incinerate the bails used during the Melbourne Test and present them, enclosed in a small earthenware urn, to Bligh after England won the third Sydney game and the rubber 2–1.

Later, however, it was revealed that the England side had spent Christmas Day and Boxing Day on the Clarke estate at Sunbury, just outside Melbourne. In the course of the Yuletide festivities, the host, his family and guests indulged in a special game of cricket, after which there was a ritual burning of the bail used in the match. Many now believe it was the ashes of this bail which were enshrined in the clay urn that now reposes in the memorial Gallery at Lord's.

But the romance of the Ashes story does not end there. After the death of Lord Darnley in 1927, the Ashes were bequeathed to the Marylebone Cricket Club. Some years later, a former maid in the Darnley household came forward with the story that one day, while dusting the Darnley lounge, she had inadvertently upset the Ashes urn, spilling its contents. She said she replaced them with the ashes from the dead fire in the hearth. The Ashes therefore may be of mundane origin, but the men who contested the games for them were not.

My own favourite personalities in the humorous

annals of Ashes cricket lived and played in the 1920s and 1950s, decades which immediately followed the two 'Great Interruptions' to the game. Men who survived the two World Wars, not knowing from one day to another whether they could ever play or bowl another ball, seemed to throw themselves into their resumed careers as though it were a bonus to life itself.

Warwick Armstrong, the skipper and 'Big Ship' of Australian cricket between 1900 and 1930 was, at more than 1.83 metres and 127 kilograms, much larger than life. He led his men to eight consecutive victories over the Auld Enemy in 1920–21. In England in the latter year he prevented Tennyson, the England captain, making an irregular declaration on the first day of the Manchester Test and then, in the confusion which followed, deliberately bowled two consecutive, and therefore unlawful, overs.

In the 1940s and '50s, the game was peopled by such characters as Lindsay Hassett, the Australian captain between 1948 and 1953. 'Tasket' was the Puck of cricket and a man of such personal charm that he could get away with the most outrageous pranks both on and off the field. A firm favourite of the late Australian Prime Minister, Robert Menzies, Lindsay often stayed with 'The Boss' in the Lodge when the PM staged his side's game against the touring team. One morning he even took the morning tea tray into the Prime Ministerial bedroom, decorating it with flowers he had pinched from the vase on the landing outside the bedroom door.

After the Sydney Test of 1954–55, Lindsay delivered a speech at the dinner on the evening before the Prime Minister's game against the MCC. In it, he declared that if England's new fast bowling sensation with the enormous run-up, Frank Tyson, dared to bowl him a bouncer on the following day, he would hook him out of sight! While he was speaking, a violent thunderstorm was raging outside the dining-room of the Canberra Rex Hotel. As 'Taskett' finished his hooking boast there was a tremendous clap of thunder and a vivid flash of lightning. Right on cue, Lindsay added: "There you are! He's started his run-up already!"

I once saw Hassett drop England opening batsman and compulsive hooker, Cyril Washbrook, twice in quick succession at deep fine leg, off Ray Lindwall. After his second miss, Hassett appropriated the helmet of a bobby patrolling the boundary and indicated that next time the ball came his way he would catch it in the headgear.

Not without justification, Sid Barnes, the Australian opening batsman of the '30s and '40s, was dubbed by his team mates the 'Artful Dodger' after Dickens' character in Oliver Twist. Sid regarded his tours of England as an excellent opportunity to set up an import-export business. To visit his hotel room, as he progressed around the country, was like stepping into an Indian bazaar. He was up to every trick of the profit-making trade. One of his schemes involved shooting a film of the 1948 tour, a film which he later showed to cricket audiences all around Australia.

When he was batting or fielding, Sid delegated his Sam Goldwyn role to one of his fellow tourists. His stand-in was shooting during the Manchester Test when Barnes, fielding in his usual suicidal short leg position, was felled by a pull shot struck with tremendous power by England pace bowler and tailend batsman, Dick Pollard.

The bolo punch took Barnes in the ribs and he

collapsed, to be borne from the field by four burly policemen. As he was carried past his fellow film producer in the Old Trafford Members' enclosure, the 'Artful Dodger' made a timely return to consciousness and demanded of his colleague in an urgent whisper: "Did you get it?" At the subsequent showings of his epic film, Sid always said the blow "would have killed an ordinary man".

Barnes, like Hassett, was a practical joker. During the First Test between England and Australia in 1946–47, Brisbane's Woolloongabba Ground was lashed by a cyclonic storm. Huge hailstones beat a tattoo on the corrugated iron roof of the wooden shed which then served as the 'Gabba pavilion. Sid deliberately stimulated the visitors' imagination with stories about previous storms and hailstones like cricket balls which hit the ground like meteors.

When his victims were in an appropriate mental state of credulity, Sid left them to watch the pyrotechnics of the storm and extracted a large block of ice from the galvanised iron bath which served as a refrigerator to cool the dressing-room drinks. Going to the rear of the pavilion, he hurled the chunk of ice over the roof so that it fell in front of the window of the English dressing-room. The Poms' eyes popped out of their heads as the enormous synthetic hailstone fell from the skies, and hit the ground with a shuddering thud!

The story of England offspinner Jim Laker's 19–wicket haul in the Old Trafford Test of 1956 was both earthy and heavenly. The earthy side lay in the dustbowl surface of the Manchester pitch, which gave the side batting last no chance of avoiding loss against a competent finger spinner.

When Aussie captain Ian Johnson lost the toss and

was asked to bat second, he realised that the match was virtually lost before it began. As he picked up the coin flipped by England skipper Peter May, 'Johnno' looked towards the pavilion and the England dressing-room. There on the balcony, freshly arrived from his pastoral duties in the East End of London, was the England No. 3, the Reverend David Sheppard, still dressed in his clerical garb.

"It isn't fair," said Johnson wryly. "Look who you've got on your side!"

When Australia and England next met on the Test field, in 1958-59, God was on the side of the big battalions. Australia certainly had might on their side— in the persons of fast bowlers Ian Meckiff and Gordon Rorke. It was a fearsome year for batsmen, the era of suspect speedsters—quickies with kinks in their actions. Of all the Australian States, Queensland alone was above suspicion. In splendid isolation in Brisbane, the legendary Ray Lindwall regarded himself as a fast bowling dinosaur: the last of the Straight Arms.

Of all the abundant suspect crop, Rorke was the most frightening. He was more than two metres tall, jerky in his action, had no idea where the ball was going and dragged his rear foot so far in his delivery stride that he cut the popping crease before placing his front foot a metre further down the pitch! For the batsman it was a terrifying sight to see this giant speedster skating towards him, without any apparent prospect of releasing the ball.

In their wisdom, the England selectors of 1958 had chosen what they regarded as one of the strongest Pommie teams ever to visit Australia. Richie Benaud's young, jerky Turks annihilated it 4-0! When young England batsman Colin Cowdrey returned home to

England and the beauty of Lord's, he was taken to task on his failure against Rorke by a venerable MCC member, a crusty old colonel of the Indian Army school. "Rorke!" snorted the peppery one from above his blood and yolk MCC tie. "In my day we would have put our front foot down the pitch and hit him back over his head. We would have charged him like the Light Brigade! Why didn't you charge Rorke, Cowdrey?"

"I couldn't sir," replied 'Kipper' Cowdrey politely. "If I had stepped forward to drive, Rorke would have stepped on my toe!"

In the past, Ashes series have been marred by such controversies as the 'chucking' debate of 1958; they have been spoiled by the real hatred engendered by the Bodyline dispute of 1932–33. In the end, however, the quality of the players who represented their countries in such matches has shone through the dross of disputation which sought to tarnish the sporting image of the Ashes tradition.

The Australian captain of the early 1900s, Monty Noble, accompanied the touring sides to England in the depression years of the '20s and '30s. Every morning he ordered a full breakfast to be served in his room—in spite of the fact that he did not eat the meal. He gave his bacon and eggs to the underpaid, undernourished chambermaids, whose lean and hungry look would have put even Cassius to shame.

Noble by name and Noble by nature.

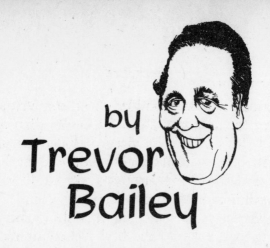

by
Trevor
Bailey

GOING UNDER DOWN UNDER

It was my good fortune to tour Australia on three occasions, providing me with a kaleidoscope of memories, both on and off the field. These include batting against Ray Lindwall, the best fast swerve bowler I encountered; surfing; bowling at the sparkling Neil Harvey; water-skiing at sunset off the South Australian coast; numerous duels with Keith Miller (Cavalier versus Roundhead) and assisting Fred Trueman to take an early bath. As a result of these tours I have enjoyed numerous happy reunions with my former opponents during five subsequent visits to the Land of Oz.

Over the years, England have made some odd selections, but few more peculiar than the MCC party chosen for the 1950–51 tour. One had a third-choice skipper, Freddy Brown (who did an outstanding job) and of the seven pure batsmen, six were openers! The theory that an offspinner would not take wickets and legspinners and left-handers were essential still existed. The result was that we set sail with a side clearly lacking in balance, as well as being short of class, to do battle with a team which had annihilated us in the two previous series.

There are advantages, however, in being written off

before a ball has been bowled. Even some Australians felt sorry for us and we did far better than anybody expected. It is true that victory eluded us until the last Test, but we could well have won the First and Second if Denis Compton had averaged 40 instead of seven, or Bill Edrich had not been left behind.

The biggest surprise to me was the quality of the umpiring in the Tests, the best I encountered in any series. Coming from a losing tourist, who always tends to be critical, that is praise indeed.

The player who intrigued me most was Jack Iverson, who bowled googlies and the occasional leg-break using

HE'LL BE RIGHT, MATE—
IT'S JUST THAT UMPIRES
AREN'T USED TO PRAISE
IN THIS COUNTRY..!

a method we had not encountered before. He could not bat, was surely the worst fielder to have represented Australia and had come straight out of junior cricket into the first class game. But, carefully handled by Lindsay Hassett, he took 21 wickets at 15.23 apiece.

The delight and surprise at dismissing Australia on a plumb pitch for 228 on the opening day of the First Test was somewhat dampened by encountering my first and only Australian 'sticky'. Twenty wickets fell for 102 runs between shortly before lunch on the third day and stumps. My satisfaction at a scoreboard reading Australia 3/0 was offset when we lost four of our second-innings wickets in the closing stages when the pitch had eased out. Those wickets included my own off a full-toss, and another, run out attempting a fourth run!

Mid-afternoon during the Fourth Test, Lindwall slipped me a bouncer. Although I dropped it dead at my feet, I made the error of doing so with my thumb instead of my bat. A visit to the hospital confirmed the thumb was broken and on my way out I was met by a photographer who asked me—me, of all people, who has been known to faint at the mere sight of a needle—if he could take a picture of the injection.

I showed him that my thumb was already in plaster, but he said it did not matter, all that was required was a nurse, a needle going into my other thumb and he would simply reverse the negative. I graciously declined.

This injury gave me an extra few weeks in Sydney, which was very good news for the oyster industry. I had already fallen in love with the local oysters and I doubt if any tourist has disposed of more.

The highlight of my second tour was England

retaining the Ashes in style. From a personal angle it was probably my best series as an all-rounder, but it again started with a disaster at the 'Gabba, where we lost by an innings and plenty.

Ironically, in the course of a prolonged occupation of the crease, I did hit a £100 six (given by a generous local businessman), which represented a tidy sum in those days. This enabled me to throw a lively party after our defeat, in the Lennons Hotel, then the best, and certainly the most civilised, in Australia. The following day a few of us not required to perform at Rockhampton flew back to Melbourne.

As we walked into the foyer of the Windsor Hotel, looking distinctly rough and feeling rougher, we encountered Robert Menzies, then Prime Minister and always a passionate lover of the game. He identified the situation instantly—"You boys could do with a grog," he said and took us up to his suite.

For neither the first time nor the last, the fate of the Ashes was decided by pace, backed up by a balanced attack, canny captaincy and some class batsmen. Frank Tyson blasted his way through the Aussie batting line-up, but I have always felt that if their selectors had included the obdurate Ken 'Slasher' Mackay instead of one of their more dashing strokemakers, the result could have been different.

Even in Adelaide, when we required only 94 on a placid pitch to retain the Ashes, the mercurial Miller had us 3/18. We eventually struggled home by five wickets.

My third and final tour of Australia was a disappointment, not so much because we lost, but because we failed to play to our potential. It was made even more disappointing personally as a bad back, which required manipulative surgery on my return to England, meant that I failed to contribute as much as I should have done, and my international career ended on the lowest possible note with a 'pair' courtesy of Ray Lindwall.

When a team is doing badly, it is useful to have an excuse, which on this occasion was provided by the number of Australian bowlers with suspect arm actions. Australia had always been rather more tolerant and this was presumably why 'Dainty' Ironmonger, back in the 1930s, was never chosen to tour England. However, in 1958 the situation was plainly out of control. Only one State, Queensland, did not include 'throw-draggers' or 'dart' players. It led to a big purge, and sadly among the victims was Ian Meckiff, one of the most delightful of men ever to have represented Australia.

Sir John Mills and his wife, who were in Australia for the shooting of *Summer of the Seventeenth Doll*, threw a real memorable party during this tour. Haley Mills, who had not yet become a child star, helped serve the drinks; Ernest Borgnine showed pictures of his wife; Tommy, an Irish cameraman, never stopped talking and, around midnight, Anne Baxter dived into the pool fully clothed. This was the signal for Fred Trueman to seize a hose and from the edge of the pool cause a certain amount of watery mayhem.

The target was irresistible. The look of utter disbelief on Fred's face as he resurfaced, in his best suit and still holding the hose, reduced me to tears. I slipped discreetly into the background and a somewhat irate Fred went on revenge, and proceeded to throw in an entirely innocent Australian actor.

It was a good night!

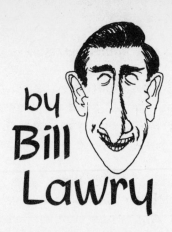

by Bill Lawry

A DIFFERENT KIND OF ASHES

In 1956, after the Australian team had lost the Ashes in England, there was a strong dose of the proverbial salt rubbed into the wounds when the Australians Cricket Board had the team play another three Tests against India on the way home.

Now to my way of thinking the tour of India was, and quite possibly still is, the greatest challenge facing a cricketer from Australia. A different way of life, more than 700 million people, tough cricket conditions, extreme heat and, for a touring captain, a nightmare trying to keep the team confident, happy and, while avoiding ulcers, stay the same yourself.

For the captain of a team touring India (yours truly in 1969–70), the rest day is a touch of heaven, or it should be! What you don't need is to have somebody hammering on your door on the rest day at 6 o'clock in the morning. The first thought that goes through your blurred mind is if it's who it was last rest day and he's pissed again, I'm going to break his bloody neck. Finally, after the usual struggle, you untangle yourself from the mosquito net, beat off the mosquitoes and it would be fair to say you are not in the best frame of mind; when you open the door and standing there in only his briefs is Graham McKenzie, the most

41

placid, gentle giant one has met, a captain's dream, never injured, never any trouble, the perfect team player, great bowler and your former room mate and friend.

Then at 6.02 a.m. he pushes the local paper in your face and screams, "What are you going to do about this?" At home at 6.02 a.m. I am down at the pigeon loft. The air is chilly, the birds are on the move, for me it's the most peaceful and enjoyable part of the day. As I let my pigeons out for exercise they circle high towards the peaking sun, and I am at peace with the world.

In India I am not so much at ease. "What the bloody hell am I going to do about what?" is my curt reply. At this point, despite the hour, I notice that the knuckles on McKenzie's right hand are turning white as he strangles the paper. My learning days at Preston Technical College come into play. I have three options— duck, slam the door in his face, or invite Graham in for a cup of tea.

Commonsense prevails. I pick up the phone and call for two teas as McKenzie opens the paper and the headlines announce "McKenzie and Redpath told to apologise or be sent home". It was a great story— McKenzie picks up local reporter and bodily throws him out of his room and down the stairs. Now, laughing merrily, though a trifle warily, I ask "Did you throw him head first, or did Redders give you a hand. Were you sober or drunk?"

At this point I realised I was getting the John Nicholls or Dennis Lillee stare which sears the eyeballs (yours not theirs) with its icy intensity, and I wonder where the hell is Fred Bennett, our manager. Team managers have the happy knack of always writing lengthy reports on our behaviour on and off the field, but when they are needed they're rarely sighted.

McKenzie grits his teeth and explains that he and Ian Redpath went to the movies last night and never even saw a reporter! For the first time in many weeks I burst out laughing: the news services would be having a field day, and back home the Redpath and McKenzie families would be having a fit. The Australian Cricket Board members will be on the phone shortly and hopefully they may find Fred Bennett. I laughed harder!

"I want an apology," demanded McKenzie. "From whom," I replied, "the newspapers or your team mates?" McKenzie leaves shaking his head. At this point Fred Bennett bursts into the room and shouts the obvious, "Mate, mate, what are we going to do about this?"

"Send home McKenzie and Redpath immediately," was my reply. "We can't tolerate this type of behaviour regardless of the pressure of this tough tour, particularly as you have just promised Guharti a Test match next tour."

Bennett spun around, headed for McKenzie and Redpath's room. I was still laughing as I wondered whether indeed there were any local pigeon farms nearby. It was in fact a wonderful morning—I could be at peace with the world.

I also wondered whether Ashley Mallett or Eric Freeman would be able to recall the happenings of the previous evening.

by
Alan
Davidson

WELL, I'LL BE STUMPED!

Playing with Wally Grout over the years was never easy. No matter how you bowled or played, he was never completely satisfied. A Harvey return six inches over or wide of the stumps was fixed by pointing his glove to the top of the bails. Normie O'Neill blasting a return back would bring the wrath of Wally to bear. Hence the nickname of 'The Griz', short for the Grizzling Grunter.

During our careers together we built up a reputation of bowler/'keeper for dismissals, although Wally would argue 'keeper/bowler.

At functions people would ask "Do you use signals?" To which my reply would be "You're joking, he can't even read or write". Wally's reply would be, "I made you, you know" or "You are my favourite medium pacer". On the field was even worse. If he thought the ball wasn't hitting the gloves hard, at the end of the over he would comment, "You're bowling well today, Ian". "My name is not Ian." Wally: "Oh, I thought you were Ian Johnson bowling slow offies." Another frequent remark: "You're so slow I'll have to stand in front of the stumps to take you."

On other occasions, due to my prematurely greying hair, he would burst into song, "The old grey mare she ain't what she used to be". The remarks, calculated to inspire, were never ending. Regardless of the taunts and compliments we did enjoy a lot of success; but the final straw was on our tour of India, 1959-60.

The president of the Indian Board had chosen a team to play us at Ahmedabad. Sam Loxton, our manager, suggested that those not playing remain at the Hotel Ritz (which it was not). The unfortunates who played arrived at the ground to find a matting pitch on a grassless expanse of outfield. The president, in speaking to and welcoming the teams prior to the match, mentioned a young fellow called Sood, one of his 'selections' (who, we were told, was a relative) whose cricket career, because of university studies, had not yet been fulfilled. Our bowlers had a good look at him, quickly realised his 'potential' and bowled very accurately onto the bat, so much so he made a splendid 73.

Compliments flowed on to the president of what a great player this chap Sood was and of his 'great potential' and how he could easily find himself playing for India before the series was over.

The next game was the Test at Bombay where Ali Baig scored 50 and 58. Madras was the following Test. Baig was omitted and Sood came in as his replacement. This Test was famous for the sawdust rolled into the surface of the pitch. Great for spin bowlers, not much use to the quicker variety.

I had two wickets when the No. 9, Sood, came in. I hadn't played at Ahmedabad so I asked Lindsay Kline, who was fielding at mid-on, "What is he, left or right, what does he do?" The reply was, "He's a right-hander and he lunges at you".

In all my years with Wally we had never signalled

one another but when I turned around there he was pointing his gloves at his chest. Being the dutiful bowler I angled across the right-hander who lunged and the ball went through to Wally. Wally was so enthusiastic he threw the ball back to me—not to first slip as usual.

The next ball, the same thing, lunge and miss and through to the 'keeper. The last ball the same again. Sood lunged at three, missed three.

As Richie was bowling the other end I took my normal short-leg position as Wally arrived. In the previous Test Wally and I had just broken the Test record of Alec Bedser and Godfrey Evans for bowler/wicket-keeper victims.

My remark to Wally was, "Well looks like another one Wal, how many catches will that make it?"

Wally: "Catches be buggered, I'm going to stump this bloke".

I reiterated several previous warnings that if he ever came up over the stumps to me I would let him have one between the eyes.

At the end of a maiden over by Richie I walked back to my mark and turned to see Wally crouched down over the stumps and having a good old laugh. I was not pleased.

I thought of the bouncer—no he has a lovely wife. Ah, but what about four byes. Wicket-keepers hate byes. Leg byes they don't mind, byes they detest. I thought four down the leg side would move him back very quickly. Then I noticed Richie at first slip moving closer—that was the last insult—so I decided to move both of them back and let fly with the fastest, widest ball straight at Richie's left knee.

Sood was too good for me. This university student with the high IQ lunged at it and fell over. The long arm of Wally went out and, in a flash, the bails were off—the shout—the umpire signalled out.

Sood stumped Grout, bowled Davidson 0, was chronicled for evermore and as if that were not humiliating enough, Wally walked up to me, tossing the ball in the air and said, "And what's more Al Pal, it didn't even spin and on this pitch and at your pace, that's almost impossible!"

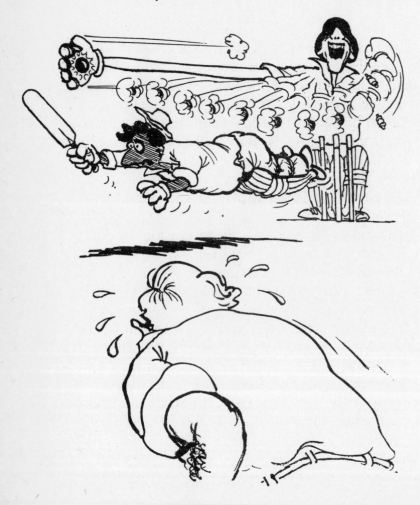

by
David
Lloyd

POMMIE BASTARDS!

I suppose it all started in the season of 1974 when I was selected to play for England in the Tests against India and Pakistan. I thought I had done quite well, a double hundred against India and a one-day hundred against Pakistan. The double hundred, I might add, was made against the ferocious pace attack of Abid Ali and Eknath Solkar, surely the quickest pair around at the time. Abid Ali, I was assured, was no relation to Bill, an Australian who played for Somerset for about 70 years.

Inevitable selection for the winter tour of Australia followed shortly and I certainly did look forward to this with some relish. I do not think I could class myself as a seasoned traveller at that time, although I had spent some time on holiday in Wales as a young boy and had also managed an odd day on excursion to the Isle of Man.

We gathered for a team talk in London and I deduced from this that our strategy in Australia would be to employ a battery of five fast bowlers to sustain the attack against the enemy, with back-up from Derek Underwood and Fred Titmus when the pitches were wet.

Our reconnaissance reports suggested to us that the

feared Australian pace bowler, Dennis Lillee, was laid up with a bad back and that a young upstart recently arrived on the scene could be disregarded as he had played in a Test match against Pakistan and returned figures of one for a hundred and plenty. The name of the chap was something like Tomkins or Timpson. First name Geoff, or Joff.

Well, it all seemed plain sailing in theory, but I suppose the first doubts surfaced when, having ascertained from the 'driver' that the plane was in fact 'roadworthy', we were informed on the intercom several hours later that we would be attacking Hong Kong sideways and on only three engines. This resulted in my first change of underwear and a further chat with the driver when I advised him to check over the plugs and tappets, which was usually the problem when my Morris Minor gave me trouble.

I was staggered that Bruce, the driver, wearing a cap with lots of braid, knew immediately this was my first time up. On landing at Darwin and stepping out of the plane, I found Bruce once more and told him the engine was overheating again. I was somewhat surprised when he informed me that "the bloody engine is fine and it's always bloody hot in Darwin, ya Pommie bastard". I must admit I really did not think that was called for.

Once we had arrived and settled in, I was eagerly looking forward to the cocktail party which had been arranged and to seeing a couple of the Aussies I had met playing cricket in the Lancashire League, 'Chappelli' and Lillee. I picked them out in the crowds and went across to say "hello". "G'day ya Pommie bastard," they replied. I said, "Ah, you must know Bruce, our driver". Blank looks followed and then they wandered off, for some reason.

On to the cricket and, after a couple of minor skirmishes which we won quite emphatically, we played Queensland, who had in their ranks the youngster Tomkins, or was it Timpson, who again bowled like a drain and we won by 46 runs. Old Timpkins would play in the Tests, we were told, and in an interview on television said he could bowl twice as fast as previously and, in his words, "I've been saving myself."

He obviously had. We lost the First Test by 166 runs with Thomson, or 'Thommo' as we came to know him, creating absolute carnage and taking nine wickets. Our strategy then was to ensure that the left-handers, and in particular the left-handed opener (which I was quickly deduced to be), took the bulk of 'Thommo's' deliveries. I doubted the wisdom of this, obviously mindful of his latest utterances on television when he said, "I love to see blood lying on the pitch". I assumed he did not mean his own.

We then sent for reinforcement in the shape of Colin Cowdrey. Colin was making his sixth tour of duty to Australia. A great man of cricket.

I opened the batting with Brian Luckhurst and Colin came in at three in the next Test match, in Perth. I had been told the pitch at the W.A.C.A. ground could be fairly pacy and, after 'Thommo's' first delivery went over my head, and then over 'Bacchus' Marsh's head, I felt that this could be one of the 'pacier' ones. After a good hour of ducking and weaving and me thinking that Thomson and Lillee were marginally quicker than Ali and Solkar, Colin came down the pitch and said the profound words, "This is rather fun, old chap, is it not?" He had flipped, I thought, and I replied, "I've been in funnier situations than this, ya Pommie bastard".

"I beg your pardon," said Colin. "I'm sorry, it's just something I've picked up from the locals," I replied. We didn't speak much after that.

I was sticking manfully to the task of looking after 'Thommo' until he struck me, bullseye, what the followers of cricket affectionately term a 'blow to the groin'. Why is it when this happens in a game of cricket everyone, but everyone, is reduced to helpless laughter and the recipient thinks that all his Christmases have come at once?

The injury did, in fact, confirm my earlier statement about 'Thommo' that I could play him with my cock, though some in the team thought it to be an extreme way of proving the point.

I was assisted from the field and took no further part in the day's proceedings. Feeling somewhat more sprightly after the day's play, I drew the short straw and had to attend the premier of a film entitled *Barry McKenzie Holds His Own*. A rather unfortunate title for a man in my delicate physical state!

The Aussie short straw was drawn by 'Thommo' who carried me into the theatre and dumped me on the stage. I really did feel like the sacrificial offering. We had a great evening, got on splendidly together and I retired for the night knowing I now had a new buddy in 'Thommo'.

I batted first wicket down next morning which, in fact, was after three balls. 'Thommo' had the nut and I took the crease with a smile on my face and "good mornings" all round. Now then, perhaps I can offer a forward defence to this first delivery from my mate, 'Thommo', I thought.

I must have been dreaming. The first ball hit me straight in the throat. The ball was retrieved by 'Thommo' himself and, to howls of laughter all round, we said in unison, "G'day ya Pommie bastard".

by Ian Chappell

CLOBBER-ED!

It annoys me that I'm often regarded as a sloppy dresser. And all because of a simple mistake I made as captain on the 1975 tour of England.

I allowed Rod Marsh to talk me into letting him open batting instead of keeping him at No. 7 in the Third Test at Headingley. I should've realised it was a move fraught with danger. It didn't take long to discover my error. By the fourth evening of the match, both Rodney and myself were out and neither would play any further part as Australia, with seven wickets in hand, chased another 225 runs.

With his Test 'over' I knew Rod would be looking for a drink, so I decided to lie low. I arrived in the Hotel lounge just after midnight to discover the 'Reverend' Rodney delivering a sermon from the pulpit. Well, that's what it looked like, as he stood, pounding the lectern with his fist as he lectured a gathering of men and women. However, there were a couple of giveaways. One, he had a bottle of beer in his other hand and two, he was saying some very irreverent things about the English cricket team. Noting that journalist and former Australian opener, Jack Fingleton, was in the audience, I decided it was time to bring the sermon to a close. 'Fingo' had once told me my swearing would get me into trouble. He'd been right. I didn't want Rodney to suffer the same fate.

"Er, 'Bacchus'," I whispered, "it's likely to be a long day tomorrow. Why don't you come upstairs and we'll have a nightcap and then get some sleep?"

"Why don't you sit down and shut up, or piss off and mind your own business," came the reply.

That approach didn't work, I thought. Better try something a bit more subtle. "'Bacchus', why don't we go drinking somewhere?" I suggested. "The casino's open late," he said, "let's go."

Delighted to have brought his sermon, which was a colourful description of how Australia would beat the bejesus out of England, to a prompt end, I didn't stop to consider the drawbacks of visiting the casino. But the problem soon became clear when at about 1.30 I suggested leaving. "Casino doesn't close 'til four," he replied as he poured another beer, "what's the hurry?" It was near five o'clock when I finally dragged myself into bed, so you can imagine I wasn't too thrilled when the phone rang at eight o'clock.

A voice said, "Quick Ian, get dressed. Some vandals have dug up the pitch and we have to go to the ground immediately."

"Piss off Fred," I said, as I recognised the voice of our manager Fred Bennett, "I don't need practical jokes at this hour. What I do need is more sleep."

"It's not a joke Ian," said the manager sternly. "I'll see you downstairs in two minutes."

I still suspected that Rod Marsh was mixed up in this matter somehow, but knowing he hadn't dug up the pitch, at least not while I was with him, I didn't have any choice. So I grabbed the clothes that were draped over a chair, slipped my feet into a pair of sandals and headed for the door. When I arrived downstairs it became obvious that Fred was serious, but there was no time to change. To make matters worse, when I arrived at the ground there were a lot of photographers gathered around the damaged pitch.

And that's how I came to be photographed in a pair of slacks, open-necked shirt, and a sweater and only a pair of Adidas slip-ons on my feet, while Tony Greig is immaculate in sportscoat, slacks, tie, shoes and socks.

BEGINNING OF THE END

In 1973–74 Dennis Lillee took the season off to try to fix his injured back for the Ashes series the following summer.

Lillee was back playing cricket for Australia in 1974–75 and ready for the Englishmen. There were also a few Englishmen who'd copped a pounding from Lillee in 1972, who were ready for him.

I had the distinct impression some of them didn't believe Lillee would ever bowl really fast again. That was their first mistake. In the opening contest at the 'Gabba, Australia batted first and England's two fastest bowlers, Bob Willis and Peter Lever, let fly with plenty of short-pitched stuff. However, when it came Dennis' turn to bat, it soon became obvious that those two believed Lillee would bowl quick again. The short stuff stopped abruptly. Annoyed at this situation Tony Greig asked for a bowl. I guess he was working on the theory that he was going to cop some short stuff from Lillee (he was right), so he might as well give a bit back. So he did. It wasn't long before Lillee was out, fending off one of Greigy's bouncers. That was England's second mistake.

Dennis stormed back to the pavilion, his anger as well disguised as a prostitute on a Kings Cross corner. As he entered the dressing-room there was an ominous quiet, which was soon shattered by the sound of Lillee's bat crashing into the metal locker. Having expelled some of his anger, he turned to face his team mates. "Just remember who started this," he said, "those bastards." Then a glint came to his eye as he added, "But we'll finish it."

And finish it he did.

OOPS, ANOTHER FIRST

Rod Marsh made his debut in the 1970–71 Ashes series. It was an inglorious start, as Rodney dropped a number of catches and earned the nickname 'Iron Gloves'. He finished his career in a blaze of glory. By then he had obtained a world record and a reputation as one of the best 'keepers of all time. His greatness was achieved by retaining a sense of humour as well as a sense of purpose. He's lost neither since retiring.

During the Bicentennial Test at the SCG in 1987–88 they were running a parallel computer Test match between two teams selected as the best from Australia and England since the war.

During intervals in the Test, scores from the computer match were flashed up on the electronic scoreboard. This created a lot of interest in the Channel Nine commentary box.

When the board displayed England's first innings score as 0/172, there were a few derisive remarks made about the 'bloody computer', but Rod was quick to come to the defence of technology. "The reason England are 0/172," he explained, "is because I dropped both Hutton and Boycott at 0. After all this is my *first* computer Test".

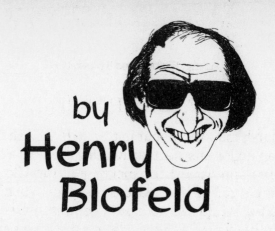

by
Henry Blofeld

THE SHOW MUST GO ON

There are certain cricket supporters who may have themselves failed to play Test cricket, narrowly in some cases, but whose presence at Test matches is more or less obligatory and more especially so when Australia is playing England.

One of the greatest and most famous of these, who possesses artistic talent by the sackful and an ability with words which 'passeth all understanding' is that irrepressible and delightful lyricist, Tim Rice.

I always feel that Test matches should not be allowed to start until he is among those present. He continues, of course, the strong and traditional link between cricket and the stage, and I am not necessarily including Mr. Dennis Lillee's more demonic methods of appealing as another such connection.

By a great piece of bad luck and, naturally, selectorial short-sightedness, Tim just failed to make the England side. One can only hope that *Jesus Christ Superstar*, *Evita* and *Chess*, to name but a hundred and thirty-eight, have provided a modest and mild form of compensation.

Thoroughly piqued by his repeated failure to catch the selectorial eye, he, like Kerry Packer before him, stamped his foot and founded his own cricket club which he, sadly and emotively, called The Heartaches. They are, I can assure you, a splendid body of men. Tim once made 49 and the principal ambition of the club is to win a match every 10 years or so.

The point of this preamble is to put flesh and blood on the great man. He did, by the way, once join the BBC's Test match special radio commentary team for a couple of World Cup matches in Pakistan and India in 1987.

He then met his self-confessed Waterloo when, after one dramatic flurry of activity out in the middle, he discovered, I think, that an England batsman had been caught by Tellerkeratne off the bowling of Wijaygunawaden which is, I agree, a set of circumstances to make strong men quail in a pronunciational sense.

Tim had three goes at it and after sounding each time like the Indian Pacific Express entering a tunnel at speed, or sundry friends of mine eating spaghetti, he discovered that the surname of one of the Sri Lankans was John.

From that moment, John had the most exhausting day of his life.

Sometimes in the same over he found himself fielding at fine leg, third man, mid-on and first slip in addition to bowling at both ends and doing a pretty nimble job with the wicket-keeping gloves on at the same time.

Now to the Ashes: we all know the acting fraternity can be vague and Tim is no exception here. When he wrote *Chess* it was with the sole purpose of opening the show in Australia during an Ashes series so that he could, as it were, kill two birds with one stone and save an airfare.

It was a long-term plan. First, *Chess* had to open

in London and then on Broadway but they don't play cricket there so he sensibly shut it pretty rapidly, and so on and so forth until the great moment arrived when it came to Australia.

But, having set up this whole course of action just to see Australia play England, or the other way round if you prefer it, which he certainly would, at the SCG, imagine what a red face he must have had when he found that the opening in Sydney coincided with a Test match between Australia and Pakistan. So much for a brilliantly conceived seven-year plan.

Now the sad thing about these chaps who write musicals is that they're as near as damn it on the breadline.

You would think wouldn't you that their pockets would be positively bulging with doubloons and pieces of eight. But not a bit of it.

Just before the opening night of *Chess* I clocked in at Lucio's, that excellent Italian hostelry in the heart of Paddington for a bit of lunch. Imagine my delight when I espied T. Rice munching away in a distant corner and we exchanged a cheery greeting or two.

He and his chum were well into their midday meal and in due course departed for other pastures. Through the window, I saw him approach a blue Mercedes and open the door—for a moment I thought he must have come up in the world, but I was disappointed to see it was his companion who climbed into the driving seat.

I was just thinking that, poor chap, he would only have been able to manage an economy class ticket over from England and what bad luck it was finding Imran Khan and not Graham Gooch in charge, when suddenly it happened.

The proprietor, almost certainly Senior Lucio himself, approached our table with an apologetic cough and in a most respectful voice asked me if I knew the gentleman who had been lunching with a lady in the corner.

I am afraid I shall have to admit that I hesitated before admitting that indeed, I did know him, for I was fearful of the consequences.

The conversation went more or less as follows:

"I don't know how to put this, sir, but he's just left the restaurant without paying the bill."

"Oh heavens," I replied, "he's done it again has he?"

"What do you mean, sir?"

"Nothing, except he's been doing it all round the world for some time now. I suppose you Aussies haven't rumbled him yet. You see, he's one of those impoverished Johnnies who write musical comedies and I hardly need add that he's desperately hard-pressed for a bob or two."

I think I probably said that, even as I spoke, he would probably be searching through a neighbouring dustbin or two for some nourishing scrap.

I was just about to reach into my pocket for a credit card and to tell the Senior that I was prepared to do the decent thing—I mean Charity begins at home and all that sort of thing—when I was interrupted by the squeal of car brakes outside, the slam of a door and the entrance at the double of a breathless, overweight, unfit, slightly red-faced but inscrutably cheerful T. Rice in person.

"Do you know," he said between frantic gasps for breath, "I've forgotten to pay the bill?"

"I do," I replied, but before I could go on he produced a bundle of the ready such as I had never seen before and I realised that for all these years I had got him wrong after all.

Tim's an old friend, a man of great generosity (and to prove that point I was the proud recipient of two tickets for the first night of *Chess*), a passionate cricket lover and, when that Sri Lankan chap John is in the thick of it, no finer commentator, although John's retirement has set Tim back a bit.

And *Chess* in Sydney was quite stunning. It moved at a furious pace quite unlike T. Rice's batting, the set was fantastic, the cast superb and the party afterwards better than that.

Now, young Tim has got to try and find an excuse to get back in time for the Ashes.

by
Derek
Randall

ANYTHING TO PLEASE MUM AND DAD

As an Englishman through and through, I was naturally gutted to see us lose the Ashes in the manner we did in 1989.

But I've little doubt the side we're now building will be good enough to regain that treasured urn the next time the Aussies are back on our soil, if we haven't already won it back in Australia in the meantime.

Ashes Tests are the greatest advertisement in the world for our sport. They are always played hard and fair and the sides generally produce some great cricketing characters, like my all-time Aussie favourite Rodney Marsh. Rodney's enthusiasm for the game epitomised the attitude of his team and you knew he'd be there behind the wicket with a few rude remarks to unsettle you every time you were out there.

I remember walking out to bat on one occasion and he was quietly waiting. Just as I thought I'd got away with it, he said, "Hey Randall! Your mother wanted a girl and your father wanted a boy. But they had you so they were both happy!"

Another great character was Dennis Lillee—a superb bowler and a great professional. He once told me he hated bowling against me. I felt quite proud because I thought it meant he regarded me as a solid batsman.

"No, it's just that I can never seem to hit you in the same place twice to pin you," he snapped back.

For one very obvious reason, I shall never forget my first trip to Australia. To make 174 in the Centenary Test in Melbourne was something beyond my wildest dreams. But I don't regard that as my greatest innings Down Under. That one must be the 150 I got in Sydney on the 1978–79 tour. It came at just the right time for me. I knew if I didn't come up with the goods I would be out on my backside. To cap it all, we went on to win that series.

Sydney, like all Australian cricket grounds, is a marvellous place to play the game. The crowds create a great atmosphere and the pace of the wickets, where the ball comes to bat, suits me down to the ground. It was pretty intimidating playing in front of those Sydney Hill fans, though.

I actually walked among the Hill crowd one day with my wife; I was soon recognised and entered into some light-hearted cricket argument. Unfortunately, one of them threw the ice-cold water from the bottom of this car fridge in my direction. My footwork was very good that day and I ducked—leaving my poor wife to take the brunt of it.

The topless beaches were among my favourite places in Australia. Not having anything quite like them at home, Bob Taylor and I would patronise them whenever we could to sit and watch the sights go by. I took in the view from under the brim of a hat and Bob through two carefully-positioned holes in his newspaper. People must have wondered why he spent hours reading the same pages!

One of the stickiest situations I got into in Australia was nowhere near a cricket wicket. Some of us met

up in a bar and we sat there drinking this concoction of whisky and icecream when in walked this stunning young lass in a short skirt. I was bet £5 I couldn't persuade her to swap tackle with me and, being game for a laugh, I approached her and explained the situation.

In no time at all I was wearing high heels, a short skirt and a pretty little hat. I was then bet another five I wouldn't dare stand outside the bar in that gear. So out I went.

A car pulled up and the bloke asked me to get in. Egged on and thinking he was part of the joke I opened the door and sat down. But as he began to pull away, I sobered up very quickly. I clocked him with my handbag and told him to stop the car or else. There was no way he was getting this maiden over!

The man who actually put me up to the bet was one Ian Botham. Now there's a man who's changed over the years! When he made his Ashes debut in 1977, he was such a gentle soul. There was no indication of the sort of larger-than-life character he was to become. But 'Both' was always an inspiration to the team. Whenever we were down, we gave the ball straight to Ian.

Another caper that sticks in the mind was Allan Lamb's first Ashes tour. When we arrived at the hotel after the long flight from England, the rest of us turned in for the night. Not 'Lamby', though. He was away on tour and wanted to have a couple of drinks in the bar. It turned out to be more, needless to say, than a sample and he was in a right old state when he got up to our room.

He was also hungry, so he called room service and began to order whatever caught his eye on the menu—

from lobster to steak .

By the time the trollies began to arrive ten minutes later, he had crashed out. I ate my fill and went to sleep. Poor 'Lamby' had a bill of about $175 to sober him up next morning.

Like a lot of other people, I was a little worried about the future of the game when Kerry Packer became involved. In retrospect there's no doubt he was very good for it. I must say, however, that our first taste of night cricket—which, of course, was a Packer innovation—had me dearly wanting to get out of the Sydney Cricket Ground.

We were practising under the lights when they suddenly went out. Our captain, Mike Brearley, remembered only then that they were set to switch off automatically at 9 p.m. We were in total darkness and it took us ages to feel our way around the perimeter to find the escape tunnel.

There was no greater feeling in cricket for me than the applause after a good innings on my home ground, Trent Bridge in Nottingham. It was a great disappointment to me, then, when I was run out by Geoff Boycott on my first Ashes game on home soil, in 1977. I suppose it was an easy way out really because the home fans were expecting me to do something special. But that disappointment passed when I took the catch that finally clinched the series at Headingley—my most treasured moment in cricket.

Back to the present day, and I reckon the current Aussies are obviously the side to beat again. They have batsmen to take any attack apart right through the middle order.

And in Terry Alderman and Mervyn Hughes (he has to be Max Walker's brother with that moustache!) they have two excellent new pace bowlers with genuine swing and pace. The only area in which I find them lacking is the spin department.

I honestly felt I was playing well enough to get into the England side for the 1989 Trent Bridge Test. However, the selectors went for youth and I couldn't argue with that.

So I imagine I will be watching the next series on television instead of from middle where I'd rather be. But as long as those who are selected wear the Three Lions on their chest with the same pride I did, then I've no doubt the Ashes will be ours again. No Worries!

by John Gleeson

COME IN SPINNER

For John Gleeson, a young, enthusiastic cricket lover from the small village of Wiangaree on the far north coast of New South Wales, Test cricket began at the 'Gabba cricket ground in Brisbane on November 26, 1954. That appearance was spent entirely in the outer, however the on-field action was to have a lasting effect on my cricket career and, indeed, my life.

On that hot, steamy morning Len Hutton won the toss and, no doubt influenced by a lively pitch on the same ground the previous week against Queensland, sent Australia in to bat. Late the first day with Arthur Morris and Neil Harvey in complete control, a spectator, having had his share of XXXX, continually called to Frank 'Typhoon' Tyson, "Come on you bloody westerly wind, blow."

Australia ran out winners by an innings and 154 runs, and confirmed what I was to learn from Tony Lock years later. In Australia, if you win the toss, nine times out of ten you bat and the tenth time you think about it, and then bat.

After the match I couldn't return home quickly enough to convey to my father my first taste of Test cricket. I would have been far wiser to have kept my mouth shut, for most of my predictions had little bearing on the remainder of the series. My biggest mistake was to say that Tyson was nothing to worry about as his 29 overs had cost 160 runs for the wicket of a youngster called Richie Benaud.

Tyson with 28 for the Test series, and Statham 18, captured 43 wickets in the final four Tests to dominate the Australian batting line-up and England ran out comfortable winners 3–1. A lesson in tact and the precarious business of predicting the outcome of a Test series on the result of one match, was well learned and heeded.

On the same ground years later I was taking part in the action this time, Bill Lawry was captain and for his own reasons had Alan Connolly bowling from the Stanley Street end and Bob Cowper from the other. By sheer coincidence they all came from the same state. I was in my normal position, leg gully for Connolly and backward of square leg for the offspinner, wondering if I would ever get a bowl.

I knew I certainly wasn't in the team for my batting. I preferred to bat No. 11—then you always had someone to walk back with; and my imitation of panther-like movement at leg gully wouldn't hold a place in any team, let alone an Australian XI.

What seemed like hours later, out of the blue came a cry from the outer, "Lawry, for goodness sake give Gleeson a bowl, he's got a grandmother who comes from Geelong." When Ian Chappell took over the captaincy from Lawry I made the fatal mistake of not telling him my other grandmother came from Glenelg!

My first 'Test' in England was in 1961 at Old Trafford, again as a spectator, as I was on a world tour with the Emu's, a northern NSW team. We had played in America and Canada before arriving in

England where we played against club sides in and
around London. We then toured Holland, Germany and
Denmark, returning home via Paris, Rome, Hong Kong
and Singapore.

After our London commitments we had a few days
spare for a sight-seeing visit to Scotland before taking
in the Fourth Test at Manchester.

For four days Australia battled after being dismissed
for 190 by an all-pace attack of Trueman, Statham,
Flavell and Dexter. With little likelihood of Australia
getting back into the game, my travelling companions
were anxious to get to Harwich on the final day of
the match, as we were scheduled to catch the ferry
to Holland early the next morning. After a long
discussion over breakfast I finally convinced our party
that we might never get another opportunity of
watching an entire Test match in England.

As it turned out we probably witnessed one of the
most exciting days of Test cricket when Australia were
rescued by a series of freakish happenings: Davidson
and McKenzie's last-wicket stand of 98, David Allen's
banishment from the bowling crease, Dexter's
electrifying 76 runs, Benaud's initiative and, perhaps,
gamble to bowl around the wicket, Grout's wicket-
keeping and Simpson's catches at first slip.

As six rather happy Emu's walked away from Old
Trafford late that afternoon one of them didn't
contemplate, even in his wildest dreams, that he would
not only return, but would play in the Test match.

I had not met Geoff Boycott before my return to
Old Trafford in 1968; however, as we took the field
he singled me out with a few words of wisdom. "Throw
'em up sunshine and I'll give you a chance."

I doubt if Geoffrey would bowl a full toss to his

granny even if it were her birthday, let alone give a cricketer in a baggy green cap an even break.

The Second Test of that series was played at Lord's where a massively built Geordie by the name of Colin Milburn struck terror into our bowling attack. He had raced to 83 when Lawry threw me the ball. I tried a planned move of bowling two orthodox offspinners, followed by a legspinner, with an offbreak action. As he went to hit the third delivery into the next county he realised too late that he was hitting against the tide and, half stopping his shot, holed out to Dougie Walters at midwicket.

The following season at Perth I played it the other way around. Two legspinners and an orthodox offspinner. The first two deliveries were of good length and line and spun nicely away from the bat. The third was the worst ball—no, the second worst . . . I'll leave that dubious honour to someone else—ever bowled in a first class game. It was so wide he somehow managed to hit it even before it bounced a second time, and he pushed it down the throat of the fieldsman at point.

As he walked past me on the way to the pavilion, with a wide grin he said, "You could bowl an orange and get me out." Sometimes the luck runs the right way.

Back at Old Trafford in 1972, perhaps I got square with my friend Boycott as I had not forgotten his statement made four years earlier. Before the Test, during a county game, I had been speaking with an umpire and he said that in his opinion I didn't appeal enough for *lbw*. Asking him how many more wickets I would have got in the match he quickly replied, "None, but gee a few were very close."

In England's second innings I hit Boycott on the pads,

TRY THIS – HE'S A SUCKER FOR ORANGES...!

and this time with panther-like speed, I spun around with both index fingers pointing to the heavens and yelling my head off. Up went Tommy Spencer's finger for both he and I knew that I never appealed unless the batsman was out.

Since that time I have run into Boycott on a number of occasions and his opening remarks are never "Good morning", "Good afternoon", or "It's nice to see you again." It is, however, a very emphatic "I wasn't out at Old Trafford, you know."

To which I would just smile inwardly to myself and know that if Tommy Spencer were present he would roar laughing!

by
Peter
Roebuck

'SAMMY'

Only one man has played Ashes cricket for Australia without ever playing a first class game on the wide, brown and empty land. His name was Samuel James Moses Woods and besides playing cricket for P. S. McDonnell's tourists of 1888 as a late replacement for S. P. Jones, who was ill, he also played rugby for England as barnstorming breakaway (Sam was built like a medium-sized oil tanker). On a brief return to Sydney in 1901–02 only a possibly diplomatic chill contracted, apparently, in a Turkish bath, prevented him assisting Archie Maclaren's team in the Test series. He was a remarkable man.

Woods was born in Ashfield, Sydney, into a family of at least 15 (Sam wasn't particular about numbers). His father was an Irishman, a martinet and an energetic fellow who made his fortune building railways and turning Manly into an important village.

As a boy, Sam played football, boxed with the local Aboriginal champion (who knelt for their bouts) and went to Fiji on a schooner to play the locals at cricket. After the first day the locals were 72/175. Until then, Sam had not realised what opposing an island meant. Ever after, he was prepared to take the rough with the smooth.

At 13, young Sam was sent to England to be educated. By the time he left school he had powerful thighs and banks of knotted muscle and a reputation as an outstanding sportsman capable of turning his hand to soccer or hockey.

Being a gentleman, Woods duly applied to attend Oxford University. Alas being a gentleman was his sole qualification for such elevation. Sam could roll a skittle, pot a billiard ball, shoot, fish, drink, sing, bowl and turn a lady's eye with the best of them. But he could not spell and so far as classical scholarship went he had a dim recollection of hearing something about a bloke called Julius Caesar and the rest was darkness. Oxford turned him away. Cambridge sport was at a low ebb. They accepted him.

Passing exams was another matter. When Sam approached the examination room, a vast figure with a shock of jet black hair and a tiny tatty gown, he was followed by half the student body, all eager that he should pass, all catching his downcast mood.

Few fancied his chances. Inside he'd bite his pen, scribble a little, then leave early, crestfallen, having perhaps written his name. Cambridge authorities managed to detect sufficient evidence of study from this to permit Woods to complete a four-year course. Cambridge won university rugby and cricket matches aplenty.

Woods stayed in England and played Test rugby and cricket for his adopted country. Besides this he went shooting (he said he had shot 'keepers and hounds in his time, though he may have been joking) and played golf, plucking beer bottles from behind trees as he went along, to the astonishment and delight of his chums.

As a cricketer he bowled fast and with great variety,

once saying that "a cove isn't bowling just because he delivers six balls to the over". He'd bowl all day, too, and was inclined to ask batsmen if they'd like it "at the heart or on the ends". As a batsman he could swing lustily and enjoyed taking harum-scarum singles which his partners did not always complete.

He had no time for draws—"they are useful only for bathing in," he reckoned—or for defeatism. Once, before batting on a sticky day, he sat sipping a double whisky and smoking a Burmese Cheroot. As wickets tumbled and his turn came, he stood up, changed into his favourite dark brown boots, shouted "This must stop!" and strode out to smash J. T. Hearne's first three deliveries over midwicket. He scored 77.

As a captain he led Somerset downhill in glorious style. A fine tactician, Sam was a less distinguished selector, largely because he liked to pack the team with his sporting chums. Once, asked to explain the appearance of a particularly incompetent colleague, he said, "Well, he ain't much of a bat, he can't bowl or field but you should see him hit a golf ball!"

He fought in the Great War, first on the Nile, a stretch of water for which he did not care. Then in Sudan, where a camel sat upon him. Finally, in Gallipoli, where he stoked fires on his ship while others fell away. Woods had been too old to fight but he went anyway.

Only once did he return to Australia. After an absence of 25 years he strode off down the gangplank, spotted his father, walked towards him, pulled out a cigar and renewed his acquaintance with the words: "Got a match, guv'nor?"

But English country life was for him. He lived in local pubs, never had two brass farthings to rub together and was immensely popular, appearing at country

"WELL, HE AIN'T MUCH OF A BAT, HE CAN'T BOWL
OR FIELD BUT YOU SHOULD SEE HIM HIT A GOLF BALL!"

cricket games, still a massive figure. He was apt to
be silent when others clapped, to then suddenly roar,
"Well played, sir!" when an edge skidded to a boundary.
He had tried to train as a surveyor, paying a man £50
to teach him. Alas this fellow returned to Bristol after
one lesson and shot himself. Roods and perches
remained a closed book. Sometimes he'd offer his
services as a doctor but since the only remedies he knew
were a wrench (for dislocated shoulders) and a double
whisky (for everything else) his ministrations were not
greatly in demand.

Apparently indestructible, Woods was at last reduced
by a crippling illness. They say his end was hurried
by a plunge into freezing water in the English Channel
to save a boy from drowning. All Somerset attended
his funeral.

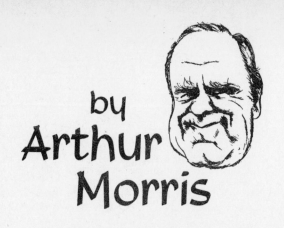

by Arthur Morris

Hey, That's MY BAT!

I never found anything particularly amusing out in the middle playing Test cricket. But after stumps, off the field, sure. There were lots of laughs and lots of fun.

For on-field humour, we could hark back to that great England player Cecil Parkin, who so loved his cricket and his county that he had his ashes spread over the county pitch when he died. A few days later, on a wettish track, a county opening bowler, who had a habit of wetting his fingers between deliveries, was heard to remark: "Blimey, old Cecil doesn't taste half bad today!"

Test cricket is grim and tough, particularly for an opening batsman, and I suppose I would have found it amusing if the opening bowler had fallen flat on his face on his run-up. However, I would not have been silly enough to laugh until I knew he had done himself an injury and was on the way back to the dressing-room.

I would never have dared do to, say Frank Tyson, what my old opening mate, Sid Barnes, did to Bill Hunt. Admittedly Bill, as bald as a badger, was a slow left-hand spinner, no threat to life or limb. Sid faced up to Bill's second delivery one day and pulled away. "What's wrong?" asked the umpire. "I can't see the

ball," said Sid. "Do you want the sight screen moved?" asked the umpire. "No," Sid replied, "make him put his cap on, the sun's shining off his bald head and I can't see the ball because of the glare!"

I understand Bill Hunt was not amused.

It wasn't the glare that unsighted me on what has become a celebrated last over of the day in a Sydney Test match against India.

I was taking strike and I called out to Bill Brown, at the other end: "I'll take the last over." It was well and truly heard by Mankad, a left-hander bowling, heaven knows why, around the wicket to me. I saw the arm come over on the second or third delivery, and I lost the ball completely. Where the hell is it, I thought. I'm too young to go blind.

I looked at Bill, who had wandered a little from his crease after seeing the bowler's arm pass the point of delivery. Mankad turned and, being in the around-the-wicket mode, took a couple of steps back, and there was the ball in his hand—running Bill out at the bowler's end. I think he said something in Indian meaning 'Gotcha' before appealing.

Bill and I, but particularly Bill, were not amused then but have had lots of laughs about it since. As I said, Test cricket is grim and tough but laughs do come after stumps and sometimes years later.

Off the field, and on it sometimes, the impish behaviour of Lindsay Hassett never ceased to amuse me.

In England in 1938, he masterminded the famous goat-in-the-bedroom trick, showing great ingenuity and courage to get a goat into Bill O'Reilly's bedroom in the middle of the night—and surviving. I was given to understand that the goat eventually ended up in

Don Bradman's room but Sir Donald would be in the best position to verify this. I'm not going to ask him.

Lindsay was irrepressible, unflappable and sometimes outrageous. But what a wonderful character.

In Richie Benaud's second Test match, in Brisbane against South Africa, we were rooming together and I suggested we have an early night. I could see Lindsay was in a playful mood so I warned Richie that in no circumstances should he answer the door if anyone knocked.

Sure enough, there came a knock, a persistent knock. Richie showed admirable restraint and I complimented him for staying in bed and not falling for the three-card trick. So off to sleep we went, feeling smug and virtuous. But things didn't work out that way because I woke to hear a familiar voice softly whispering in my ear: "Here's a nice cold beer for you." I sat up, turned to Richie, who was standing nearby and said, "How the hell did he get in?"

"Well," said Richie, "I was fast asleep and the phone rang and the voice at the other end said someone's knocking on your door. Would you please open it. So I did, sorry about that."

Ah well, I thought, he'll learn. And I did enjoy the beer Lindsay had brought me.

It was in Brisbane again, with Lindsay as captain and me vice-captain, that we arrived late for dinner, just the two of us, after a Test match. There were only three people left in the dining-room. They were speaking in a strange language as they continually tossed down these colourless drinks. One was Russian, the other two Scandinavians, dispatching vodkas in fine Russian style. Intrigued by it all, we joined them.

The Russian, who was from the Soviet Embassy in

Canberra, had very limited English. He kept repeating, after introduction: "I kom from Canberra, Mr. Hassett from Melbourne, Mr. Morris from Sydney. God friends." And that, between toasts, appeared to be the limit of his English. But Lindsay wanted some answers. So he asked about Communism. Our friend answered: "I kom from Canberra, Mr. Hassett from Melbourne, Mr. Morris from Sydney. God friends."

Then Lindsay put in the cruncher: "Do you believe in God?" "Yes," he replied, "god friends. I kom from Canberra . . ." And there seemed to be the hint of a twitch in the corners of his mouth.

Jeez, I thought, he's either the smartest Russian bear in the business or his English is lousier than I thought.

I knew the Russian was smarter than the average bear when I walked past him in the foyer next morning, and he said, "Good morning Mr. Morris."

Many years later, in 1959, after we had both retired from first class cricket, Lindsay and I played together in a Prime Minister's XI against England.

I had retired from the first class scene in 1955, but after a few seasons of no cricket at all, I returned to the district competition. I had even bought a bat, and such a good bat it was that I was making plenty of runs for my then district team, Paddington. I rarely let that bat out of my sight.

I opened for the Prime Minister's XI and hit the ball well. I scored 79, even managing to take four fours from one over from Ted Dexter. He must have been impressed because I overheard him say to Colin Cowdrey: "Who is this old bastard?"

When I got back to the dressing-room, rather well pleased with myself, Lindsay came in and asked if anyone could lend him a bat. Still on a high, and knowing that after all those years of no cricket, he could do little damage to my beautiful and much-treasured bat, I said: "Of course, old fellow—have mine."

When he went out to bat, I was standing with Richie Benaud and the Prime Minister, Sir Robert Menzies. The Prime Minister was a great admirer of Lindsay. He admired him as a cricketer and was genuinely fond of him as a person.

Lindsay, as I'd anticipated, didn't last long in the middle, despite some valiant efforts by the English lads to give him a few runs. I saw him get out and turned to Richie to comment about old cricketers hanging up their boots. Then I heard Sir Robert say, "How typical of Hassett, what a charming gesture—he really is the most wonderful man." I turned to him and asked "What happened, Sir?"

"Didn't you see?" the Prime Minister replied, "Lindsay, as generous as ever, has given his bat to a little boy in the crowd!"

"*His* bat!" I yelled, throwing protocol to the wind. "Pigs arse, it was *my* bloody bat!"

I didn't find it at all funny, especially when the boy came in the dressing-room and got all our autographs on that wonderful piece of willow. I can still see the look of adoration on the lad's face as Lindsay, with a flourish and a quick glance at me, signed his name and said: "And Mr. Morris would certainly love to sign it for you . . ."

It was vintage Lindsay Hassett, and no one could remain at odds with him for long. A wonderful, remarkable and kindly man. My life was the richer for knowing him and playing with him and against him.

He was a brilliant batsman and a splendid ambassador as Australian vice-captain to Bradman from 1946–48 and then as captain against England, West Indies and South Africa until he retired in 1953.

I was proud to be vice-captain to him. One day he might make it into Australia's Sporting Hall of Fame, but I'm not holding my breath!

My last words on Ashes humour or Ashes fun come from that great England fast bowler, Harold Larwood. I spoke to him on the phone recently and he wondered if the players enjoyed their tours these days, with so much more cricket to play.

He mentioned he'd introduced himself years ago to Geoffrey Boycott at the SCG nets. "Pleased to meet you, Harold," said Geoffrey. "Are you enjoying your tour out here, Geoffrey?" Harold asked. To which Boycott replied: "I didn't come out here to enjoy myself. I came out to play cricket."

"Oh," Harold said to me, "they've changed since my day!"

C'MON AUSSIE C'MON

by
Keith
Stackpole

THE FIRST LESSON

It used to be said that the Ashes Tests were *the* Tests. If you played in those, and succeeded to boot, then you were rated as having made it on the international cricket scene.

I've got no doubt that Australian cricketers still rate the Ashes as the premier series to play in and that the 1989 triumphant Australians under Allan Border will cherish that success for the rest of their lives.

I say that even though it is clear all of the other Test playing nations have improved their game dramatically over the past decade and there is little difference between them in playing standards.

It's just that there's a sort of notoriety attached to Ashes tussles; England is the enemy to be beaten at all costs. No Aussie cricketer worth his salt would even think of losing a Test, let alone a series, to England.

I remember I was 16 when Jim Laker, the great England offspinner, took those 19 wickets in a Test against Australia at Old Trafford, and for weeks afterwards I was distraught, unable to comprehend how one man could wreak such destruction and virtually beat Australia on his own.

During those formative years of my life in cricket everything seemed so serious about the game whether

87

I was watching from over the boundary fence, on television, listening on the radio, or reading about it in the paper. So you can imagine my intensity when in only my second Test match, I faced England at the Melbourne Cricket Ground.

England won the toss and batted even though the pitch looked to have something in it for the bowlers. The England openers were Geoff Boycott and a stroke-making left-hander, Bob Barber.

Australia's great speedster Graham McKenzie bowled beautifully, continually beating the outside edge of the tentative Barber's bat. Naturally this was very frustrating for the expectant Australian slips fieldsmen who were doing plenty of 'oohing' and 'aaahing'.

Wally Grout was the Australian wicket-keeper with captain Bob Simpson alongside him at first slip and myself at second slip. 'Garth' McKenzie sent down another beauty which again beat Barber. 'Oooh', 'aaah'. And Grout sent the ball on its way back to McKenzie, via the field.

As a confident 26-year-old I eased over from my spot at second slip and told Grout and 'Simmo', "This bloke cannot bat."

Grout went a sort of red colour in the face and his eyes blazed as he exploded, "Hey son, how many Tests have you played in? Keep your stupid comments to yourself."

Boy, was I looking for somewhere to hide! At the end of the over when we were walking down to the other end, Grout spoke to me again. He could see I was upset and this advice was delivered less sternly and more fatherly. "Just look after yourself and don't worry about mouthing off opinions about others until you've made the grade yourself." Then at the end of the day's play he again sought me out. "What did you learn today?" he asked.

"Plenty," I replied, "but I'm going to keep it to myself."

DO-IT-YOURSELF CRICKET

In 1966 I went to England to play in the highly-rated Lancashire League, where I was the professional for the Ramsbottom club. In my first four innings I made 0, 0, 8, 0, hardly what the club's administration had been hoping for.

My fifth innings was to be played against Rishton whose professional was the much-respected and experienced Johnny Wardle, who had played for England. But heavy rain prior to the game had left the pitch, uncovered in those days, saturated.

This was of little consequence to Wardle, who upon arriving demanded, "Well, what time do we start?" There wasn't even a pitch prepared. Wardle said, "Look lads, I've not driven 50 miles for nothing; we are going to have a game of cricket."

He then proceeded to the groundsman's shed and came out pushing a handmower. Thirty minutes later we were playing on a very soft, very suspicious pitch cut by none other than Wardle himself! To roll it would have been a waste of time, the roller would have bogged.

Rishton won the toss and batted, Wardle reasoning the pitch could only get more difficult as it dried out.

I bowled medium pace and when Rishton lost their third wicket at 35 Wardle came in. It was professional versus professional.

My first ball to Wardle was straight at the middle stump and on a good length. He aimed a mighty swipe likely to hit the ball not just for six over the fence but surely out into the main street of the town some way off. However he miscued badly and the ball flew high in the air to my left. I sensed it would fall between the fieldsman at mid-on, a local named Peter Ashworth, and yours truly.

To this day I can still hear 'Ashy' calling "Mine, mine!" It was a call so full of confidence that I left it to him. To my amazement he never laid a finger on it. In fact he was so far out in his calculations he allowed Wardle through for a single!

As the tough old 'pro' Wardle ambled past me he offered, "Hey lad, when you're the 'pro' do it yourself, never leave it to these stupid idiots."

He had a bit more advice for me after I collected another duck when I batted. "As soon as you get to a ground make a point of going and introducing yourself to the umpires. You know, get them on side a bit, lad."

I knew my Sheffield Shield captain back in Australia would have frowned on that bit of gamesmanship. Bill Lawry was his name. But I was in desperate trouble, four ducks in five digs.

Next match, as soon as I got to the ground, I went straight to the umpires' room and introduced myself. I noticed then, and on every other occasion I went to the room, they would always ask, "What do you think of the standard of League umpiring?"

Now I was a product of a Christian Brothers College

and therefore found it downright difficult to tell lies. But on these occasions I have to confess to a few white lies.

"Great," I'd say. "In fact it's not all that far below Test standard." And I'd swear I could see their chests puff with the pride of a peacock.

Anyway, later in the season we played Bacup and batted first. I still wasn't seeing the ball all that well but had reached double figures when the bowler dropped in a bouncer.

Seems the word had even travelled across the world ... "Stackpole's a sucker for the pull shot". Because this bloke was quite a bit slower than the first class bowlers his bouncer more or less sat up and begged to be hit.

I pinned my ears back and with a full swing of the bat and a grunt tried mighty hard to hit it to the boundary. But because it came off the pitch so slowly I was almost through with my shot by the time the ball reached me.

Instead of connecting with the middle of the bat the ball merely brushed my glove and was caught by the wicket-keeper. The Bacup boys appealed, jumping around, for the catch, but to their amazement, and mine I might add, the umpire said "not out".

The Bacup boys were ropable. In the Leagues it's common knowledge that if you get the 'pro' cheaply you'll nearly always win the game. Anyhow I scored a single off the next delivery and copped an earful from the bowler who was still muttering obscenities as he walked on back to his mark.

The umpire who had just given me not out moved over to me. He whispered, "You got a little glove on that one before, did you?"

I felt obliged to tell the truth. "Yes," I admitted, "but why on earth did you give me not out?"

He gave me a bit of a smile and said, "Well, you seem such a nice bloke to be having such a bad trot, so I thought I'd give you a bit of start today".

SNOWSTORM

When I was playing Test cricket the spirit of the game was such that you made many friends out of the game and even came to admire many of your so-called enemies. One such 'enemy' was John Snow, the England speedster.

'Snowy' got me out eight times in Test matches, three more than any other bowler. But even though we were tough opponents we also had a great respect for each other, and over the years a rapport built up between us.

Once, in a One-day encounter at Lord's, 'Snowy' greeted me with "Not you again, you big fat bastard!"

To which I replied, "I hope you're not going to bowl that crap to me today, 'Snowy'!"

It was another encounter with John Snow that led to an unusual reaction from an umpire on Australia's tour of England in 1972. In the first three Tests of that series I was dropped five times off snicks behind the wicket.

The fact was my defensive technique was not quite good enough for English pitches where the ball tended to move around a great deal. Still, I had what I thought was a fair theory. I reasoned that if I was going to snick the ball then I should get plenty of bat on it to ensure the catch heading for those fieldsmen behind the wicket was not an easy one.

In the Fourth Test, which was at Headingley, a ground where the ball seemed to move more than any other, we batted first. Sure enough I went for a big drive early on against John Snow but succeeded only in getting a sharp edge which fairly flew through the slips for four.

One of the umpires was David Constant, then the No. 1 umpire in England. At the end of the over, he moved in from square leg and came and stood next to me.

He said, "You are the arsiest batsman I've ever seen!" Now I've never been lost for a word, particularly to an umpire. I said, "David, at least I'm good enough to get an edge on them. Have a look at your blokes, Luckhurst, Boycott, Edrich and Mike Smith trying to play Dennis Lillee . . . they aren't good enough to even get an edge."

This was the infamous 'fuserium' Test when the pitch took spin from the very first morning. The pitch was as bare as The Great Sandy Desert, a condition that was blamed on a disease, or fungus, called 'fuserium' which was apparently caused by prolonged rain before the Test.

Even so when England batted, although most of the bowling was done by our spinners Ashley Mallett and John Inverarity, they did have to face 20 or more overs from Lillee.

After one Lillee over Constant came up to me with a smile spreading across his face and said, "You know, you're right—a couple of them are not good enough to get an edge".

C'MON AUSSIE C'MON

by
Neil Hawke

. . . BUT WHOSE CHAMPAGNE?

Unwittingly and most unwillingly, I was soon to become part of Ashes, in fact cricket, history.

In 1964 the great Freddie Trueman stood on the brink of the magical 300 Test victims, a milestone no bowler had ever accomplished. In the Third Test at Headingley, bolstered by some rough treatment of the England bowlers by Peter Burge, in company with the Aussie tail, we got off our knees and won a Test we had no right to win. Tantalisingly poised on 297 wickets, Trueman was omitted from the Fourth Test at Old Trafford when both teams' first innings extended beyond 600.

Sitting with the great man at Old Trafford, he reminded me of his objective and, even though the team for the final Test at The Oval had yet to be named, Fred announced he would be playing. I said, "If you want one for 300, when I come in, I'll see you get it. It's the only way they'll remember me." Fred replied, "If you do sunshine, you're on a bottle of champagne."

With Fred having a reputation of giving away boomerangs and homing pigeons, I certainly wasn't going to hold my breath.

England batted first and had made 60 for the loss of only Bob Barber; I grabbed six wickets as England were shot out for 182. Included among those was Fred.

When he took guard I anticipated he might just throw the bat at the first ball to show up the batsmen who had fallen cheaply before him. I reasoned a slower ball might tempt him into a lofted shot. It certainly did but he made rather better contact than I anticipated and the ball bounced once before disappearing over the pickets. Fred, pleased with himself, did a lap of honour and paused in front of me to say, "Thanks sunshine, I'll see you get one to get off it".

FS made 14 before Ian Redpath caught him off me, and our batsmen passed England's 182 with only three wickets down.

England fans watched and waited as we steadily built up to a very strong position. With six wickets down just before lunch on the third day Fred remained wicketless. With his captain, Ted Dexter, practising a few nine irons on the midwicket boundary, I suspect it was Fred who put himself back on to bowl.

It was a good change because Fred's fourth delivery penetrated Ian Redpath's watchful defence and bowled him. 298! The very next ball Graham McKenzie edged an outswinger into Colin Cowdrey's safe hands at first slip. 299! Unbelievably I was next in, now facing a hat-trick and what we had talked about in Manchester had eventuated.

Mercifully lunch was taken after McKenzie's dismissal and few left their seats as they waited for history to evolve. I felt a very lonely person as I walked out to the wicket with Tom Veivers. Fred was polishing the ball vigorously as I walked past him at the pavilion end. "You'll now get one to get off it lad," said Fred.

I was shaking too much to take guard and all sorts of thoughts rushed through my mind as Fred came

charging in. Perhaps he had stiffened up during lunch because he strayed wide outside off stump. For 40 minutes Tom and I denied him his special moment until I edged him straight to Cowdrey and gave him the first of the many handshakes he would receive that August day.

He completed the day with 301 wickets and, true to his word, walked into the Australian dressing-room and gave me a bottle of champagne.

Later on, one of Fred's team mates said, "Nice gesture from Harry Secombe to send FS a dozen bottles of champagne".

MAN AND WIFE . . . AND STRIFE

When Australia were dismissed for 78 in reply to England 7/351 declared in a rain-ruined Second Test at Lord's in 1968, there was a story behind the story.

Bob Gray, the Sydney *Mirror* cricket correspondent, had chosen the Sunday rest day to marry his beautiful West Indian sweetheart, Grace. They had a central London apartment at which the team, fellow journalists and close friends had gathered.

Gray and another couple of apartment tenants had a common entrance key, but Gray, having mislaid his own key, had no means of re-entering. Nor had the wedding guests. Undaunted, he knocked on the door of the lower flat, the tenant of which stood wide-eyed and open-mouthed as she surveyed this strange collection of human beings. Gray said, "My name is Robert Gray and I am the tenant on the second floor. I'm just popping off down the road to get married and I've lost my front door key. I'll be back in about half an hour and would you be kind enough to let me in when I ring the bell?"

The wedding ceremony featured a casual, relaxed groom, more intent on checking his watch than repeating wedding vows.

Returning to the apartment, there was the challenging sight of a bathtub full of bottles of champagne, which were covered to the corks with ice.

It was a challenge most of us met with some relish, although skipper Bill Lawry sensibly stayed teetotal and concentrated on the orange juice and beautifully made smoked salmon sandwiches.

The following day Lawry and Ian Redpath strode to the middle to take block on a pitch which, after overnight rain, had sweated badly under the covers. Wickets tumbled. Lawry at 1, Redpath at 12, Cowper at 23 and only Doug Walters (26) and John Gleeson (14) reached double figures. The other batsmen struggled to come to terms with the movement of the ball in the air and off the pitch, Barry Jarman sustained a broken finger and there was an eyebrow or two raised over whether the Gray wedding festivities had any effect on the less than brilliant performance.

All was saved for Gray though when we battled back to save the match with 4/127 in the second innings, with just a touch of assistance from the weather.

It is still known among the players as 'Gray's Test'.

CAUGHT OUT

When Bob Simpson and Bill Lawry opened the Australian innings with 201 at Manchester in 1964 a big total was inevitable. Simpson went on to score 311 in Australia's 8/656 declared. England replied with 611 with Ken Barrington (256) and Ted Dexter (174) scoring the bulk of the runs, the latter century after a very strange reprieve.

On 108 he scooped a ball up to point and the heavily-built Peter Burge dived forward and appeared to slide his hands cleanly beneath the ball and complete a catch. Ted seemed to think so and, tucking his bat under his arm, turned and strode towards the pavilion.

He covered ten yards when he paused, turned and said, "Oh I say Peter, did you catch it?" Burge, caught off guard by this eloquent and civilised enquiry answered in like fashion, "Well Ted, I really don't know".

We then looked at umpire Syd Buller. He simply said, "Well if he doesn't know if he caught it we had better play on".

Thus I was denied my only wicket in 63 overs, 28 of which were maidens with 95 runs conceded.

In the same innings genial offspinner Tom Veivers was asked by Bob Simpson to bowl the first over of the final day so that Graham McKenzie and I could change ends. The fifth delivery pitched outside off stump, turned sharply, lifted and flew over Barrington's shoulder and straight to the boundary for four. It was the only ball that had done anything unpredictable, and for the first time we had the sniff of some batting discomfort.

Veivers bowled on and on unchanged until the

innings closed, finishing with 3/155 off 95.1 overs. Ironically, following that one freak delivery, the pitch played as predictably as it had on the first day.

Bill Lawry is a very single-minded man. As a captain he didn't really believe in fraternising with the 'enemy'. We were at cross purposes in this as I had always believed it was possible to enjoy a good relationship with opposing players and still be hard and worthy combatants.

Colin Cowdrey, a gifted batsman, is a warm and affable man. As he walked out to bat against us at Lord's in 1968, I was near the stumps and I said, "Good morning 'Kipper' ".

"And good morning to you, 'Hawkeye'," came the cheery reply.

I thought I detected a long, hard look from 'Phanto' but it was only after I had spent several overs trudging from fine leg to fine leg that I realised how easy it is for a captain to make a point to a player without actually saying anything!

by Norman O'Neill

CHAMPAGNE CRICKET!

The 1955–56 cricket season in Australia was very special for me. It provided my greatest thrill in sport. The five New South Wales selectors, in their wisdom, included me in the 12 to play South Australia at the Sydney Cricket Ground.

I was 18 and at the time it seemed like only yesterday that I had sat in the Sheridan Stand watching my idol Keith Miller carve up the opposition, scoring brilliant centuries and causing the opposing batsmen all sorts of problems when he had the ball.

Only those who have experienced the uncomfortable feeling of being in the same dressing-room as their idol all-time greats could realise how I felt back then in 1955–56. The dream had come true for me; I had achieved the first part of my obsession. To wear the blue cap of NSW was a stepping stone to the green and gold of Australia.

I have no idea if the players of today are encouraged in the same way as the youngsters were in my time. But I do know that my eventual promotion to Test level was assisted considerably by my peers. The first time I attended a first class training session, I felt I should have been wearing an identification tag. Yet I had the pleasant experience of having one, Richie

Benaud—a man I had only seen and admired from afar—extend his hand without introduction, call me by name and wish me well. From that day Richie played a significant role in my future as a NSW and Australian cricketer. He also became a very good friend.

I was 12th man in my debut match. Richie made 51 and took 6/76, but that's not the reason I recall the game so vividly. It is because Keith Miller bowled out South Australia for 27, which was the lowest total in Sheffield Shield for 72 years.

It was a well-grassed pitch and NSW made just over 200 before Miller declared. Warren Saunders, my St. George club captain in Sydney, top-scored with 66. Miller closed the innings and I can still remember how livid he was when the umpires granted South Australian openers, Favell and Harris, the light after they had made two runs without loss.

The next morning Keith was late and Richie had to lead NSW out. Keith was late because he had forgotten to pick up Peter Philpott at Manly and had to do a U-turn on the Sydney Harbour Bridge and dash back for him.

We managed to delay things long enough for Keith, laces flapping and tucking in his shirt, to bowl the first over of the day. That was the end of it! You've never seen such a procession. South Australia were all out for 27. Batting again, South Australia had got to 0/12, which must have seemed odd for anybody arriving at the ground just before lunch.

NSW continued their dominance of the Sheffield Shield competition that season. We played eight matches and I participated in seven of them, six as 12th man. In the other, I batted only once and was clean-bowled without scoring. So much for my first class career, I thought—but the encouragement from my team mates persisted.

In March, 1956, the Australian team led by Ian Johnson left by ship for England and we knew they had a great chance of returning with the Ashes. Like all lovers of the game, I followed the Ashes series night by night on radio. It was with disbelief that I awoke one morning to hear that, to go with his nine wickets in Australia's first innings of the Fourth Test at Manchester, Jim Laker had taken all 10 wickets in the second and the Ashes would certainly not accompany the Australian team home.

I very clearly recall reading the reports in the newspapers that day and must confess the photographs and newsreels of the 15,000 people standing and cheering the victorious Englishmen as they popped champagne corks into the crowd, left a feeling of emptiness. It was at that moment I decided that more than anything else I wanted Australia to regain those Ashes and never let them slip through our fingers again. To an Australian cricketer or cricket fan, the most important thing is to whip the Poms. It has always been that way and always will be.

And so it was that in 1961 we docked at Tilbury to renew hostilities. Newspaper reports indicated this was one of the poorest Australian teams ever to land on English shores. Can you imagine such a reckless description of a team which included Richie Benaud (as captain), Neil Harvey, Alan Davidson, Bob Simpson, Ken Mackay, Colin McDonald, Peter Burge and Brian Booth? Not to mention the then-unknown Bill Lawry.

We won at Lord's, with Neil Harvey as captain, and were beaten at Headingley on an astonishingly-prepared pitch. Old Trafford, Manchester, was to be the most important match of the series. We had to win to retain the Ashes, which we had so convincingly regained in 1958 in Australia. To lose here would send us into the Fifth Test at The Oval with a 2–1 deficit and very little chance of squaring the series.

It was a magnificent game of cricket and fortunes fluctuated throughout the match. Between lunch and tea on the final day, victory in the match and the series certainly seemed to belong to England. I shall never forget Neil Harvey saying to me as we walked to our positions in the covers: "We need a miracle, Normie. We've got to win here. It'll be a flat pitch at The Oval."

The miracle happened. Richie Benaud changed his direction to bowl around the wicket to Ted Dexter, into footmarks created by Freddie Trueman, Jack Flavell and Dexter himself. He kept landing the ball on those footmarks and so outstandingly did he bowl he finished with 6/70 against a world-class batting line-up.

Alan Davidson sent Brian Statham's stump flying with 20 minutes to go to wrap up the England innings and it was with a certain amount of disbelief that we walked from the ground, the Ashes retained.

When we reached the dressing-room we were greeted by our manager, Syd Webb, and assistant manager, Ray Steele, who apologised that the champagne hadn't arrived. We understood because only a couple of hours earlier the caterers had been scheduled to deliver it to the England dressing-room.

As we sat around chuckling over what had just happened, I looked at Benaud, Harvey, Davidson and McDonald and it seemed they were quietly lapping up the satisfaction of sweet revenge. They were showing little emotion, but they were loving it.

My own thoughts flashed back to that fateful day

in 1956. I remembered the photographs and the newsreels of the English team standing on the balcony popping champagne corks into the crowd of 15,000 cheering below.

Just ten minutes after the game had finished Ray Steele handed each of the 17 players in the touring party a bottle of champagne. He suggested that in the true spirit of Australian sportsmanship we should appear on the balcony, pop our corks and acknowledge our success and, if possible, thank the vast crowd for the true sportsmanship they had shown throughout the series.

The balcony doors were opened and out we went, champagne bottles in hand and broad grins on our faces. We looked down upon the huge crowd below, the throng who had come to salute the victors. What we saw was one man. He wore a grey dustcoat and carried a stick with a spike on one end. He was picking up litter.

I looked hesitantly at the 1956 brigade—and at that moment they burst out laughing. Victory was sweet for all of us that day; to them, it was nectar.

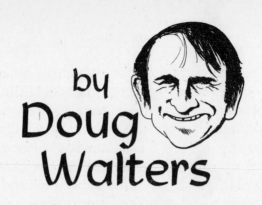

by
Doug
Walters

My Roomie Les Joslin

My first tour with an Australian team was to England in 1968. It was the first trip away for quite a few players, Victorians Paul Sheahan and Les Joslin among them. Bill Lawry was captain and Bob Parish our manager and they decided on the room pairings for the tour. I was a relative newcomer to cricket and I guess neither Bill nor Bob knew a great deal about me or some of the other rookies.

I certainly wasn't going to complain about their choice of room mate for me. I was delighted to be touring, having just finished two years' national service training which had meant sharing rooms and tents with all sorts of people from all walks of life. The name Les Joslin sounded pretty good to me as keys were handed out. I had no reason to think any differently at any stage of the following months. Here at least was one player who got value for the money the Australian Cricket Board laid out on accommodation during the tour. Les was a non-smoking teetotaller, which made us a bit like the odd couple. Unlike the television series or movie, however, neither of us were worried by the habits of the other.

The first week of the tour was spent practising at Lord's between showers of rain and attending numerous official luncheons and dinners which go hand-in-hand with all Ashes tours. After the first week, the fact that our attendance was still often required at official functions and that the usual attire was a dinner suit, was starting to become somewhat tiresome; but I remained optimistic and looked on the occasions as a free meal (thus saving on my allowance) and a chance to sample some of the nice French wines which were served as an accompaniment. My room mate, of course, didn't share in any of the wines and just couldn't wait for the cricket matches to start.

The Duke of Norfolk traditionally hosts the first match at Arundel Castle. It was a bleak day and we needed as many pullovers as we could possibly fit into and still move. As newcomers, Les and I were equipped with only one sleeveless and one longsleeve jumper, so we still froze.

Once the cricket part of the tour was under way, I saw a very conscientious room mate. If there were no official functions, Les was in bed every night at eight, so keen was he to do well. It was a problem, because the sun doesn't go down in England until 9.30, but once in bed, Les would write a letter home and then read one of the many thick books he had packed for the tour.

I was often surprised when I would creep into the room considerably later than 9.30 and find him still reading away with his bed light on. I started off by remarking that it must be a great book but Les said it was nothing special. He couldn't sleep, he confided, because he was wondering what the bowlers were going to deliver in his direction the next day.

After this had happened several times, I urged Les to join me along with a few of the other fellows down in the bar before trying to sleep. He was immoved by my entreaties, even though they became very frequent as the weeks went by.

As the tour progressed, it became more and more evident that Les was having a miserable time. He had worried himself out more times than the bowlers got him. Les didn't play first class cricket very long after that tour. In fact, his career included only one Test match.

Many years later, I was doing a promotion for Tooheys 2.2 beer in a hotel in Melbourne when I came across the new Les Joslin. As I walked into a crowded bar, someone shouted "Hey 'Bikki'" (that being my old nickname prior to being known as Fred). My ears pricked, but there was so much noise and so many people elbow to elbow I couldn't work out who had called. Again I heard, "Hey 'Bikki'". I looked across to the adjoining bar and saw a fellow with a schooner in his hand waving to me.

He was a big fellow, about 17 stone, I saw. He didn't look familiar, but I made my way over. As I got close enough to say hello I recognised the face but still couldn't remember who it was. He put out his hand and said, "Les Joslin!"

I stared. My he *had* put on weight, but that shouldn't have surprised me because many people do that, particularly sportsmen who are no longer training. But this man was holding a beer in one hand and a cigarette in the other. Nothing added up to the Les Joslin I had shared a room with for almost six months in 1968.

"Great to see you," I said, shaking his hand. "I wish I'd taken your advice years ago," he said, pointing to his beer. "And I work for Philip Morris these days," explaining the cigarette.

We reminisced a while; it was quite obvious that the new Les Joslin was thoroughly enjoying life. I've wondered since whether Les would have scored more runs if he'd been more relaxed during that English tour.

Tell you what—falling to sleep at night wouldn't have been the same problem!

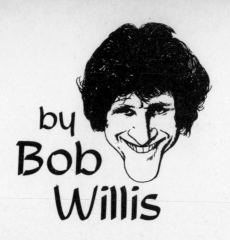

by Bob Willis

BETTER THAN AVERAGE(S)

Throughout my career, the most meaningful international games were always those against the old enemy, Australia. They were also the most enjoyable—full of hard, unrelenting, high-pressure cricket but with a culture and humour between the players of both sides. There was always a beer available at close of play, when both combatants would sit down and tell a few tales and pull a few legs.

There is no doubt in my mind that Test cricket was devalued in the years 1977-79 because men like Dennis Lillee, Rod Marsh and Greg Chappell were off the scene playing World Series Cricket. When they returned to the Test fold, they stuffed us 3-0 in 1979-80, but at least it was good to be back against the genuine articles again.

Inevitably, funny moments kept crowding in on me in my dotage as I sat thinking about all those momentous games with the Ashes at stake. On my first trip to Australia, in 1970-71, I was instantly struck by the hospitality of the home fans despite the inconvenience of their being so far away from the essential amenities.

Generously, they proffered a drink to the young, skinny fast bowler as I stood, perspiring, on the boundary. Only after I had raised the can to my lips and tasted the warm, salty liquid did it dawn on me that I'd fallen for a typical piece of Australian spectator humour!

I think they took to me straight away, though. On my first appearance for England out here, I was greeted with a hospitable message from the crowd: "Hey Willis! I didn't know they stacked crap that high!" I wasn't the only Pom to be the butt of Aussie humour, though: "Hey Underwood! You're so slow you can read the adverts while you're running after the bloody ball!"

The Australian press did not shirk from a few pithy descriptions of me, either. When John Snow was physically attacked on the boundary at Sydney after he had hit Terry Jenner with a bouncer, I went down to give him moral support as the crowd mood turned ugly. Bill O'Reilly, that great character who was writing for the *Sydney Morning Herald* at the time, was fairly unimpressed by my physical presence. He wrote that I would have been pretty useless in the event of physical ructions because I looked like a two-iron with ears. I reckon old Bill got me about right.

If you were an England cricketer, you certainly needed a sense of humour to deal with the Aussie umpires. Some of them occasionally needed the white cane and a guide dog. Others were so disarmingly open about their defects that it was hard to get really annoyed at them.

Take Mel Johnson, for instance. In the crucial Sydney Test of the 1982-83 tour, we needed an early breakthrough to have any hope of retaining the Ashes. It came in my first over when I ran out John Dyson with a direct hit. He was out by something like six feet. In fact, when the ball hit the stumps he wasn't even in the action replay frame on television. For some reason, umpire Johnson gave Dyson not out. When I raised a quizzical eye at his decision, he said: "Sorry, but I always give the batsman the benefit of the doubt if it's a matter of six inches."

I ought to have known better because the game umpire had shown similar flexibility in the 1974-75 tour, when I had Queensland's opener plumb low with the first ball of the match. Not out. Mel's comment to me at lunchtime was: "I'm like a batsman, Bob— I like to get my eye in early on."

If we couldn't always understand the Aussie umpires, we had to say the same about our own Derek Randall. Now Derek was one of the greatest characters of my time—a genuine, scatter-brained, highly-strung original. All the England players dreaded sharing a room with him on tour because he could never relax.

Ian Botham tells a brilliant story about Derek going out for a walk at Sydney the night before he was due to bat in the 1979 Test and proceeding to get lost. Ian had just got back from the hotel bar about four o'clock in the morning when Derek staggered in, totally sober but in a panic because he hadn't been able to remember which hotel he was at. And when he'd stopped passers-by to ask them, they'd given him a very strange look and shied away.

Randall then bullied Botham into having a cup of tea, switched on all the lights, plus the television and radio, all the while singing at the top of his voice. They finally got to sleep about six o'clock—and then Randall went out and scored 150 in the fiercest heat imaginable.

Only Randall could take the wrong turn as he came off the field at the Melbourne Cricket Ground after scoring 174 in the 1977 Centenary Test—and find himself face to face with the Queen. A perky "howdya do" to his monarch and he shuffled off in the opposite direction.

Derek used to drive Rod Marsh and the Aussie slip

fielders to distraction with his non-stop chattering to himself. It would be something along the lines of "Hey oop, Rags, it's a nice day, lovely wicket, now don't get out. Concentrate, concentrate". All very well, but he said all this as the bowler was running up! Eventually Marshy and the close fielders put cottonwool in their ears when Randall was batting because they couldn't stand the din. He was one Englishman who definitely didn't get worried about sledging!

I suppose my greatest memory of contests against the Aussies must be that astonishing Test at Leeds in 1981 when we came back from the dead to win against all odds. Well, 500/1 in fact—and congrats to Rod Marsh and Dennis Lillee for managing to get a bet on while still in the field. Bob Taylor tried to get out of the England dressing-room to put some money on, but he couldn't get through hordes of autograph-hunters. Marsh and Dennis were shrewd enough to delegate the task to their 12th man.

That is a fairly well-known story about Leeds '81, but few people know that the boys of the England team had said a slightly inebriated farewell to each other on the Saturday night. We had assembled at Ian Botham's house for his traditional Leeds Test party (he lived about fifty miles from Leeds in those days) and we were all certain we would lose at some stage on the Monday. So we decided to climb into the booze to drown our sorrows.

We knew that the press would be on our backs on Monday and that, for some of us, it would be the last time we would play for England. I certainly included myself in that category and I believe Ian thought he might be rested as well. The general feeling was that this eleven would not be playing together again for our country, so most of us had a few.

I vaguely remember dancing with Botham at some stage. The rest, as they say, is history, thanks to Botham's 149 not out and 8/43 from yours truly—but we would have been useless if we'd had to play on the Sunday!

Great times, great friendships—with the Aussie players as well as the English boys. As one of the more serious, intense England cricketers of that period, it took me a long time to relax and enjoy the peripheral aspects of Test cricket, but now I treasure the laughs and the companionship more than any statistical achievements.

They can always be put into perspective, but the fun has been bottled, racked up and is occasionally uncorked.

by
Dennis
Lillee

MISTAKEN IDENTITY

The most unexpected drama can happen on a cricket tour. Generally it relates to player problems but in this particular case during a tour of England in 1972 I was the subject of some over-zealous English cricket fans wanting revenge. Back in the 1970–71 tour of Australia, Graham McKenzie, playing in a One-day fixture between the Gillette Cup winners Western Australia and England on a bad Sydney pitch, broke Geoff Boycott's arm with a ball which took off from a good length.

Those avid fans thought I had been responsible and during our Test match at Trent Bridge in Nottingham decided it was time to get hold of the culprit and give him his just deserts. Most of the team had gone out in small groups for a wholesome meal at the end of this particular day's play and as another group in which Bob Massie was present arrived inside the foyer of the team hotel, five or so of these self-appointed vigilanties looked at Massie and said, "There's Lillee, let's get him!" Bob, thinking of his own skin yelled back, "Like hell I am," and rushed out of the foyer to the safety of his room. Despite the truck load of booze this group of English fans had on board, they realised their mistake and continued their vigil outside the hotel foyer.

Later, fired up with a few more ales the group entered the foyer and attempted to find my room number through the services of the night porter. He quickly realised they had had too much to drink, should not have been in the hotel and asked them to leave immediately. For his trouble the poor guy received a broken hand and a busted watch as he evicted them and locked the front doors.

Meanwhile Bob Massie had gone upstairs and asked the players where I was. They said I hadn't arrived as yet, and several of the players were sitting in my room looking out of the window to warn me, and the other players with whom I'd had dinner, that a group of Pommie supporters were after my skin.

While they were waiting our group came in the hotel back entrance. As I opened my door I don't know who got more of a shock, me seeing people hurriedly scatter in the darkened room, or them, thinking I was the ringleader of the group who might have found a way into the hotel.

PROMISES, PROMISES

The 1974–75 MCG tour to Australia is one most Poms wish to forget as Australia completely outshone England in all departments to record a 5–1 victory in the series. It was a series which the Poms felt very confident of winning as the Australian pace bowling stocks were very low. 'Thommo' had played one Test the previous summer against the Pakis, registering 0/100 on the flat MCG pitch, albeit playing with a broken toe! Consequently, he wasn't even considered a threat by the English press. I had been out of all cricket for nearly two years and this was my comeback.

The first leg of the attempted comeback was in Adelaide against South Australia. Watching from the sidelines as I again entered first class cricket, were most of the English players and press. I can tell you I didn't do a lot to instil fear in their hearts as I went about my task very gingerly and with little success.

However, 'Thommo' and I made the First Test team and bowled England out with some extremely fiery and dangerous bowling. This was especially true of 'Thommo' who bowled like the wind and had all the Poms either digging out rocket-like 'sand-shoe crushers', rearing bouncers or short-pitched deliveries.

All batsmen were troubled by this tornado who they had not even heard of before the tour commenced. One who copped a hell of a time of it was a terrific guy and a solid left-hand opening batsman called David Lloyd. I can still visualise the new ball flying past his nose at nigh on 100 miles per hour, leaving him all at sea against 'Thommo'. Short of a length bowling with nothing much up to drive was sending him mad. His letters home contained paragraphs of his nightmares against this continual barrage.

One such note to his Mum summed it up perfectly. "I know I promised I'd hit a boundary in front of the wicket Mum, but so far I've failed. I've done more ducking and weaving than the guys I've watched in the boxing ring out here with the Aussie champion Tony Mundine, but for one instant I thought today was the day to keep my promise. I got a half volley from 'Thommo'. Trouble was I'd forgotten what a half volley was and I only patted it back down the pitch."

G'DAY . . . G'D GOD!

Of course it is commonly known that Paul Hogan immortalised the Aussie way of saying hello in the form of G'day, but a young and inexperienced Australian fast bowler, on his first Ashes tour to England in 1972, became very infamous to all his team mates and to royalty through that very shortened slang term.

We had been invited as a team to visit Buckingham Palace for afternoon tea and, of course, to be presented to Her Majesty, the Queen. What an occasion. To say I was nervous was an enormous understatement.

Our manager, Ray Steele, had enjoyed the opportunity of being presented to the Queen a couple of times before as an official of an Australian team so he was an old hand at the required etiquette. I must say listening to him explain the course of events and what to say and what not to say or do was very confusing. I thought, in the end though, I had worked it out.

Ray Steele introduced the team members to H. R. H. The Duke of Edinburgh one by one and, as is protocol on such occasions, Ian Chappell as captain introduced them to H. M. The Queen. As my turn came and the Queen stopped in front of me I must have slipped into panic mode. We looked at one another for a few moments until I just pushed out my hand and said "G'day".

Bob Massie on my immediate right and Rod Marsh, who was next to have the honour of meeting the Queen, could not control themselves and laughed quite uncontrollably at my faux pas. I survived but to this day have not been allowed to forget that most embarrassing moment of my life.

A few minutes later Ian Chappell sought out Ray Steele and said to him, " 'Cast', you wouldn't guess what Dennis said when I introduced him to the Queen".

"Yes I would," Ray said, "G'day, exactly the same as he said to the bloody Duke!"

So 'Hoges' maybe you will have to give me some credit for immortalising the catch cry 'G'day'.

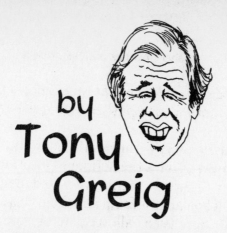

by Tony Greig

BLESS YOU 'BACCHUS'!

The Centenary Test in Melbourne in 1977 was a momentous occasion by any standard. The celebrations which marked 100 years of Test cricket between England and Australia were both memorable and lavish. Some great individual performances saw records tumble and, by a freak coincidence, Australia's winning margin was 45 runs—exactly the same as in the first-ever Test between the two countries.

It was none of these things, however, or even the fact that I had the honour of captaining England, which made this such a memorable match for me.

As in any Test, there was tension—and this was no ordinary match! It was certainly not incident-free, but one particular happening ensured the Centenary Test would always be something special when I looked back down memory lane. The incident in question demonstrated a number of things to me. It showed clearly that even the best umpires are far from infallible; that the frustrations of captaincy can and do make mere mortals of a group with an image of perfect gentlemen; and that a magnificent sportsmanship survives in this great game of ours.

After low scoring first innings by both sides, Australia declared at 9/419 in their second, leaving us to make

463 runs for victory—57 more than had ever been scored in the fourth innings by the winning side in any Test. Understandably, we weren't given much of a chance. We batted well, however, and at one stage it seemed as though we might pull off what would have been an incredible victory.

When I joined Derek Randall at the crease, England were 5/346. Randall was batting magnificently and with supreme confidence, and I was feeling in good form. Australia's bowlers had all worked extremely hard, but at this stage they were visibly tiring and Australia were struggling. That much was obvious to anyone with normal eyesight and hearing. In the circumstances, captain Greg Chappell decided to bowl himself and, with Randall on 161, it all happened.

Chappell got one to nip back at Randall and, as I saw it, the ball flicked his left pad and flew through to Rodney Marsh behind the stumps. Frustrated like the rest of the Australians, Chappell appealed—pleaded would probably be a better description—to umpire Tom Brooks for a catch at the wicket.

To my own and Randall's utter astonishment, Brooks gave him out. I hasten to add that Brooks is one of the fairest men I have ever met, but I was convinced he had made a wrong decision on this occasion.

Randall, obviously stunned, paused for a few seconds before starting his long walk back to the MCG dressing-room. He had gone about five metres when Marsh, who had tumbled over in taking the ball, called out to Randall: "Come back!" He indicated that the ball hadn't carried to his gloves and had hit the ground first.

Again I was amazed. The match was at a critical stage and Marsh's action could well have changed the

outcome. Further, I had always been convinced the Australian philosophy in a situation such as this was to accept the umpire's decision whether they believed it to be right or wrong.

The action of Marsh—the supposedly uncompromising, tough guy of Aussie cricket—came as a real surprise and provided great pleasure. It was a thoroughly sporting gesture which was accepted by Brooks, who promptly reversed his original decision. A splendid performance all round by everyone concerned, although I'm not 100 per cent certain Greg Chappell viewed it in precisely that same light (until he cooled down)!

England's tour of Australia in 1974–75 was the toughest Ashes series in my time. When we first arrived in Australia, Dennis Lillee had broken down with a serious back injury and few people outside Australia had heard of Jeff Thomson. Overseas, they couldn't even spell his name correctly. The situation was soon to change dramatically.

Our batsmen took a dreadful hammering during the First Test in Brisbane. David Lloyd had a finger broken and, despite the lack of any positive X-ray evidence, John Edrich was convinced he had more than one broken rib. Personally, I believed Edrich, as he was undoubtedly one of the toughest opening batsmen I had the pleasure of playing with or against.

In the circumstances, we had no option but to send for a replacement and, after considering all the alternatives, we decided on Colin Cowdrey, who had watched the Brisbane Test from the comfort of his couch at his home in Kent, with snow lying thick outside.

This was the first tour of Australia Cowdrey had missed in 20 years, but he would have been excused for expressing a preference for his lounge room in Kent rather than facing Lillee and Thomson in Perth. But, when the phone rang and he was asked to report to Heathrow without delay and be ready to play in the Second Test on the fastest, bounciest pitch in the world at the W.A.C.A. in a few days, he was on his way.

Cowdrey, rising 42, arrived at the ground by taxi dressed in a typical City of London pin-striped business suit and with, like all Englishmen in mid-winter, a particularly pale complexion. I shall never forget Max Walker's reaction as the roly-poly figure of Cowdrey alighted from his cab. " 'Thommo' and Lillee will kill him stone dead!" he said.

When I joined him at the crease in that Test, Cowdrey had been there for about an hour. The first ball he had received from Thomson was in Rodney Marsh's gloves before he had started his attempted pull shot. He had taken numerous body blows and had only managed to compile nine runs. Cowdrey, however, was a classical cricketer and a master of the art of building an innings.

In contrast, I had adopted a much more aggressive policy and put the first three balls I received over the heads of the slip cordon for four. At the end of the over, I was 12 not out and had already overtaken Cowdrey.

When we met in the middle of the pitch for the customary chat between overs, I looked at Cowdrey, feeling almost apologetic, and explained that what he had just witnessed was part of my new-style method against 'Thommo' and Lillee. I asked him politely not to try to change my thinking.

His reply was a classic. "Interesting. Very interesting. Just keep going, son." And with that he turned and walked back to his end.

C'MON AUSSIE C'MON

by Dickie Bird

A BIRD'S EYE VIEW

How nice to be invited to contribute to a book about Ashes humour. I've stood in many series between England and Australia, so I've seen a lot of great games and a lot of funny things that have happened in the course of them.

Don't let anyone ever tell you that cricket umpires are without a sense of fun. He may wear a straight face out there on the field most of the time, but believe me, we enjoy cricket's lighter moments as much as anyone. We may not initiate those moments of folly and farce, but we are so often drawn into them. Umpiring can be a very funny business indeed.

Whenever I reflect on Ashes fun and games, the name Dennis Lillee recurs. And why shouldn't it? In his long career as Australia's incomparable strike bowler, we had much dialogue.

During a test at The Oval, Dennis threw the ball to me mid-over and said quite matter-of-factly: "It's out of shape." I looked at the ball and replied: "It's all right. Keep on bowling, it will knock itself back into shape."

"Well I'm not going to finish the over, so they'll not get a chance to knock it back into shape," said Dennis.

I was firm. "I'm not going to change that ball."

So was he: "Then what are we going to do? I'm not budging!"

"Well, we might as well sit down," I said.

So, in the middle of a session of the fourth day's play in the Fourth Test between England and Australia at The Oval in 1975, we all sat down. I don't know what the radio and TV commentators made of it, or the press. There was no mention of a sit down strike in the newspapers next day.

The ball was in a bad way, but I didn't propose to change it in the middle of an over. At that time the public were getting fed up with continual inspection of cricket balls. Hardly a ball seemed to last its allotted 85 overs. Dennis had been chipping away at this particular one for some time. He'd been toiling on a slow pitch against an England side who were merely intent on surviving.

Ian Chappell, the Australian captain, came up. "What's the trouble?" he asked. I replied, "Ian, Dennis won't finish the over unless we change the ball, and I told him to get on with it. We'll change it at the end of the over". Ian Chappell never liked to be called "skipper" or "captain" which is the usual style of address among English sides. If anyone called him "skipper" he would reply: "My name is Ian."

"Come on Dennis," he said. "Get on with your bowling." Lillee is an independent character, but he wouldn't defy an instruction from his captain. "All right then," he said. "I'll finish the over—but I'll bowl offspinners." He got up, walked back a few yards, ambled in and bowled the perfect off-break, on a length and turning just a little. His next three deliveries to finish the over were exactly the same.

"Now Dickie, what do you think of that then?" he

said. I told him I thought he had a career ahead of him as a spin bowler when he no longer wanted to bowl fast! He handed me the old ball. It was in terrible shape and we replaced it. I hadn't changed it in the middle of the over because it sometimes happens that the ball does get knocked back into shape, particularly when a fast bowler is operating.

I produced the new ball—well, not brand new, but a ball that had been used for a similar number of overs in the nets. Dennis said with a smile: "Thanks very much, Dickie."

I had never known a bowler refuse to bowl in a Test before. I was asked later what would have happened had Chappell supported Lillee. Would the Test have been abandoned? My answer was that I didn't think it would have come to that. Ian would not have wanted to throw all that hard work away. England saved the match by making 536 in their second innings in reply to Australia's 9/532, and Lillee took 4/91 off 52 overs.

It was a most praiseworthy piece of bowling. Dennis received no encouragement from the pitch or the conditions but kept at it for more than two days. He was one of the few fast bowlers whose control was such that he could accurately predict what his next ball was going to do.

In that same match he said to me: "I'm going to bowl an off-cutter and it will rap him on the pads, and I'll be up for an appeal. You watch!" He ran up and bowled an off-cutter which rapped the batsman on the pads. But I spoiled it for him by turning down the appeal. We had quite a chat. He was pretty talkative on the field.

Along, I suppose, with every other student and lover of cricket, I regard Dennis as one of the greatest fast bowlers of all time, and Ian Chappell as one of the greatest captains. In my experience, the Australians have always played cricket the way we play it in Yorkshire—very hard and competitively, and occasionally with some needle. Like the Yorkshiremen, they play to win and don't like losing.

Umpiring in a Test match at Old Trafford once, Bob Holland was bowling from my end to Graham Gooch. Graham hit a full toss like a bullet—and straight at me. It hit me right on the ankle and down I went. On to the field came the Australian physio to give me treatment. He came on to a tremendous roar from a full Old Trafford house.

After the treatment, Holland thanked me for saving four runs. Gooch was livid because I'd robbed him of four runs. It is amazing what can happen in the middle in a Test match, and how different attitudes can apply.

I was in the Australian dressing-room at The Oval at the end of the final Test of the 1975 series, when Dennis Lillee presented me with his official tour tie. With it was a note saying, "Thanks for everything, from Dennis and the boys". He had autographed the tie with: "Best wishes, Dennis Lillee." I have that tie on display at home. Money could not buy it. It shows I had the respect of some of the world's most competitive cricketers. I couldn't have wished for a higher recommendation.

Most Australians have a sense of humour on the field and Dennis and Rodney Marsh were prime examples. They inspired a very successful practical joke at my expense during the Old Trafford Test in 1981. As I prepared to leave the umpires' room for the start of play, I heard a conversation in the doorway. Some of the Australians had pushed their way in. I ushered them out and, suspecting something was 'going on', returned to the room to check that everything was intact.

When I put my hand in my pocket, it closed around something strange. It was a snake. I screamed, hurled it across the floor and fled, calling to the attendant: "There's a snake in there! For heaven's sake get rid of it!"

Dennis and Rodney were very perky throughout the first session. They kept asking me if everything was all right and insisting that I looked a little out of sorts. "I'm all right," I said, "I'm all right, quite all right". I got on with the morning's play, trying to put the matter of the snake out of my mind. Nevertheless, I still felt very apprehensive when the luncheon adjournment arrived.

I was definitely ready for a break, if only to steady my nerves. The soup bowls were already on the tables when we arrived in the dining-room and they had little metal covers to keep the contents warm. I lifted the lid on mine without thinking, and there was that confounded snake again!

I cleared the danger zone at high speed, and when I reached the safety of the corridor, I could hear the roars of laughter behind me. Dennis and Rodney followed me out. The snake, they said, was made of rubber. I didn't bother to confirm it.

Cricket has been very good to me. It has given me the chance to see the world and meet some wonderful people. I always enjoy going to Australia when I get the chance. I have made some wonderful friends there and they all treat me like a king.

I hope I will be around for a few more years with my white cap. Hopefully, I shall not be needing a white cane to go with it.

by
Brian Johnston

IT'S THE ASHES! IT'S THE ASHES!

I have commentated on 75 Tests between England and Australia—either on TV or radio, so the Ashes have played quite a big part of my life.

I first heard of them in 1921 when I read about Gregory and McDonald blockbustering the England batsmen, including my hero Patsy Hendren who made 0, 7, 0, 10 and was not surprisingly dropped. I was also slightly surprised to see a photograph showing a large man *on* the field at The Oval, resting against the pavilion rails *reading a newspaper!* Not cricket I thought. It was Warwick Armstrong registering his boredom at the English batsmen, who at last were actually making some runs.

Five years later I was listening on a cat's whisker wireless to a report at the end of the Fifth Test at The Oval where England had won and regained the Ashes. There was of course no commentary from the ground in those days, so Patsy Hendren was rushed to Broadcasting House in a taxi. I have always remembered what he said: "The Oval crowd were real glad, and all was merry and bright." Short, accurate and a model for our modern summarisers!

I saw my first Test at Lord's in 1930, where Percy Chapman made a brilliant 121, hitting Grimmett for four giant sixes into the corner of the Mound Stand. I also had my first sight of Don Bradman, though he only made 1, out to an amazing low catch by Chapman in the gully.

I next saw Bradman and Australia at Lord's in 1938 where Wally Hammond slaughtered poor Fleetwood-Smith in his great innings of 240. I missed seeing Hutton's 364 at The Oval but listened to the burbling commentary of Howard Marshall.

After the war I became a TV commentator for the BBC and so was privileged to watch and admire that great 1948 Australian side—the best ever to come to England.

We had to wait until 1953 before we regained the Ashes in the Fifth Test at The Oval. It was a great moment for England. Australia had held them for 19 years. I was lucky to be commentating at the end. With five runs needed for victory, Lindsay Hassett put on Arthur Morris with his left arm chinamen from the pavilion end. Bill Edrich got a single, then off the fourth ball Denis Compton swept Morris to leg. The crowd rushed on, thinking it would be certain four. But Alan Davidson at short leg stuck out his great claw and stopped the ball. There was a delay whilst the crowd went back, then the next ball was outside the leg stump and Denis swept it to the square leg boundary. Whether it ever got there no one will ever know, as the crowd rushed on to the ground and enveloped the players. Edrich and Compton forced their way back to the pavilion with bats held aloft, just like submarine periscopes. I shall always remember this match. I can still hear my raucous cry of "It's the Ashes, It's the Ashes," as England won. I'm afraid I sounded a bit too pleased for an unbiased commentary, but after all it had been 19 years since the Ashes were back in England.

There were happy and lively celebrations in the England dressing-room, in which, sportingly, the Australians joined. I'm afraid the dressing-room clock got the worst of an encounter with a bottle of champagne. Jim Laker was so elated that he went off to see South Pacific and only realised when he went backstage after the show that he had arranged to meet his wife Lilly at the back of the pavilion at 6 p.m.

In 1953 I made the first of my many gaffes. It was at Headingley, Australia were fielding and the TV camera panned in to show Neil Harvey at leg slip. Without thinking I said: "That's Neil Harvey at leg slip, with his legs wide apart waiting for a tickle."

It was also during this match that a man walked past our commentary box carrying a ladder over his shoulder and a lavatory seat round his neck. Jim Swanton was commentating and deliberately stuck to the cricket and made no comment on this extraordinary sight. It was even more extraordinary when the man returned ten minutes later with the ladder but *minus the seat*. Where had he put it that needed a ladder?

As in 1953 I was again lucky to be on the air when England regained the Ashes in Sydney in 1971—this time after 12 years. I was so excited that I went all poetical and wrote a song to celebrate the victory. It went to the tune of an old music hall song which Don Wilson and I used to sing called "Show Me Your Winkle Tonight"!

Back in England the team recorded the song. I wish I could say that it made the hit parade. It didn't. We made exactly £53.86, to be divided between us. So we decided to have a draw and asked Ray Illingworth to make it. He promptly drew out his own name! There's nowt like these Yorkshire folk.

Here are the words, which perhaps explain why it never became a No. 1 hit!

We've brought the Ashes back home
We've got them here in the Urn
The Aussies had had them 12 years
So it was about our turn
But oh! What a tough fight
It's been in the dazzling sunlight
In spite of the boos of the mob on the Hill
We've won by two matches to nil.

When we arrived people said
The Aussies would leave us for dead
But we knew we would prove them wrong
And that's why we're singing this song
Oh! The feeling is great
For losing is something we hate
So Sydney we thank you for both of our wins
But not for those bottles and tins.

Our openers gave us a good start
And the others then all played their part
We usually made a good score
Seven times three hundred or more
The Aussies however were apt
To collapse at the drop of a hat
If they were bowled any ball that was short
It was ten to one they'd be caught.

In the field it was often too hot
So sometimes we felt very low
Whether rain was forecast or not
We always knew we'd have Snow

So now to go home we are free
Though the series has been a long uphill climb
We've all had a real bumper time.

The Lord's Test 1975 saw the first ever Test match streaker. This time I was luckily *not* on the air. I would probably have got the sack. But John Arlott dealt with it with perfect wit and good taste. Alan Knott was at the non striker's end, when the streaker ran towards him from the pavilion end and hurdled the stumps. He told me later it was the first time he had ever seen *two* balls coming down the pitch at the same time.

A friend of mine, the late Les Bailey of Barnsley, sent me an appropriate poem.

He ran on in his birthday attire
And set all the ladies afire
But when he came to the stumps
He misjudged his jumps
Now he sings in the Luton Girl's Choir.

Long may the fight for the Ashes continue, but I would just like to know one thing for certain. Are the Ashes in the Urn at Lord's the same original Ashes collected by those Australian ladies from a burned bail in 1883?

I only ask because of that ugly rumour that when they were in Lord Darnley's house before he died and bequeathed them to Lord's, there was a slight accident. A parlour maid dusting the mantelpiece knocked the Urn off, and the ashes scattered all over the carpet. So she simply took some ashes from the log fire, popped them into the urn and put it back on the mantelpiece.

I wonder if anyone has ever inspected and tested them. Wouldn't you love to know?

HE RAN ON IN HIS BIRTHDAY ATTIRE
AND SET ALL THE LADIES AFIRE
BUT WHEN HE CAME TO THE STUMPS
HE MISJUDGED HIS JUMPS
NOW HE SINGS IN THE LUTON GIRLS' CHOIR

LES BAILEY,
BARNSLEY, UK

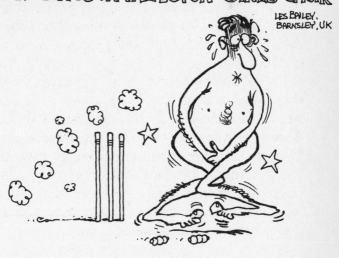

by
Ian
Redpath

THE GREAT MAN

He was a great bowler, was F. S. Trueman. He had a good outswinger, good pace, accuracy and stamina and a top memory to go with it. The first four attributes were the reason he captured a record 307 Test wickets— and he could remember every one of them!

It was ten years after the event that I saw Fred again and after about two minutes the conversation was somehow channelled towards his record. Now, anyone who has played against, or listened to, Fred knows he's never bowled a straight ball in his life and in a flash he said, "I remember you 'Redders', you were number 298. It was a lovely ball, just moved away through the air a little then cut back through the gate and hit off stump". He was spot on, except it hit middle.

There is no doubt he was a great bowler and there is no doubt also that the word modesty was unknown to him.

As the conversation progressed we got around to his career and his numerous disagreements that he'd had with the authorities. These had apparently been quite bitter and had led to him missing a game or two. Suddenly he paused and reflected on this for a moment and then quickly announced, "You know 'Redpatch', I'd have got 400 bloody Test wickets if they'd played me in the bloody games they should have!"

ROYAL COCKTAIL PARTY

One of the traditions of a tour to England was a cocktail party at Clarence House given by the Queen Mother. The Queen Mother has a deserved reputation of being a very natural and friendly person and on these occasions many of her family also attended, much to the delight of the touring party.

The manager of the 1961 tourists was Mr. Syd Webb Q.C. A delightful character, Syd, who found the many cocktail parties to be one of his fortes. After a few whiskies at these functions, Syd became suitably relaxed and, as the Royal function progressed, a couple of mischief-makers in the touring party were slowly adding 'trinkets' to Syd's suit coat pocket. By the end of the gathering Syd was everybody's friend and was quite oblivious to the fact that he had about eight and a half ounces of Royal Household cutlery, worth about 850 pounds sterling a fork, in his coat pocket.

The Queen Mother who has a great sense of humour had been given the word by the pranksters and at the end of the night, after Syd had delivered his thank you speech, the Queen Mother was heard to say, "It's been a pleasure Mr. Webb".

Just at that moment one of the team who'd been lurking close by, hit Syd's pocket which tinkled like a cutlery drawer. Syd dived his hand into his pocket and came out with a handful of the valuables.

"That bloody Lawry," cried the red-faced Syd as he visualised himself spending the rest of the tour in the Tower of London!

SIR DONALD'S PROTÉGÉ

Bobby Simpson had broken his left forearm during an interstate game against Queensland at the start of the 1965–66 season and was forced to miss the First Test in Brisbane and I was selected as his replacement. Brian Booth, the acting captain, won the toss and elected to bat. Bill Lawry and I opened and, after a breezy innings of 17 in one and a half hours, during which I had outscored Bill 2 to 1, I attempted to hook David Brown, the England opening bowler, but only succeeded in putting more glove than bat on the ball. The ball popped up and I watched in disgust as it came down right on top of the leg bail.

On returning to the pavilion and after having shed all the batting necessities, I found myself sitting next to the Chairman of Selectors, Sir Donald Bradman. This was a very perceptive man and he could see he was seated next to a disconsolate youngster who had just seen the possibility of his immediate Test career being terminated.

"Bad luck Ian," he said, "but that innings reminded me very much of one I played back in 1938". I thought, Gee, my 17 must have been a real cameo; it must have looked great from up here. Perhaps I'm still in with a chance to play in the next Test after all.

"Yes," he went on, "I attempted to hook the fast bowler, got a glove to the ball, it popped up and dropped right on top of the leg bail, just like today".

The next Test I was back playing for Victoria!

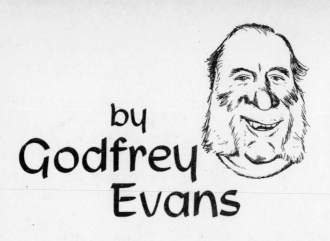

by Godfrey Evans

NEVER STUMPED FOR A CHUCKLE

To play a Test match against Australia is every English cricketer's ambition. Having played in all the series from 1946 to 1958, I can recall many episodes which still give me a chuckle.

One such occasion was during my first Test in Australia, in Sydney, way back in 1946–47, when that tough little character Bill Edrich went into bat against the fearsome pace of Ray Lindwall and Keith Miller. His journey to the wicket indicated that he'd enjoyed a very good night out.

It was one of the pluckiest innings I have ever seen. His hooking and his on-driving were superb, as was his ability to duck some vicious bouncers. He really did look safe out there in the middle and after taking his score to 110, it came as quite a surprise to see him bowled.

He came into the dressing-room, had a drink and a shower and, when he had settled down, I asked him: "What happened to get you out, Bill? You were playing so well."

"Godders, old boy," he replied, "do you think I might have sobered up?"

During the same match Australia were in a bit of trouble against Alec Bedser after a shower of rain had

HIS JOURNEY TO THE WICKET INDICATED THAT HE'S ENJOYED A VERY GOOD NIGHT OUT...

livened up the wicket. Sid Barnes was playing a very subdued role, and Don Bradman was holding himself back in the batting order until the wicket had eased. Sid was appealing against the light after nearly every ball to waste time, even though the sun was still shining. In those days, the umpires had to consult each time an appeal was made. Eventually the umpires agreed to come off, much to the delight of the Australians.

Next day was Sunday—a rest day—and by the time play resumed on Monday, the wicket had dried out into a real beauty.

At the fall of the next wicket, in came The Don. Well, he and Sid had a run feast, putting on more than 400 runs together. Bradman was out for 234 and a little later Sid was dismissed for precisely the same score.

Opening a drink after the end of the day's play, I said to Sid, "What a coincidence, you both scored 234". "Coincidence my foot," said Sid. "I got out on purpose. If I'd scored less, or even more, than Don Bradman, no one would have remembered my score. As it is now, I will be remembered because I got exactly the same score as Australia's best and most popular batsman!"

It was the Fourth Test at Adelaide and the temperature was well over the century for the duration of it. In fact, it was so hot in the hotel that Wally Hammond, our captain, told us we could stay privately with any friends if they could offer cooler accommodation. Don Bradman had introduced me to a lovely family who had a house at West Beach. Mark and Olga Lodge and their three daughters gave us a splendid time. It must have done me good because I managed to hold off the Australian attack for 95 minutes before I opened my score. Denis Compton, at the other end, completed his second century of the match.

It was during this innings, when I was facing to bowling, that Bradman brought all the fielders in close, rather like bees around a honey pot. When it was Denis to face, Don directed all the outfielders to the furthermost points of the boundary.

This strategy made Denis very angry, and I can see him now having a go at the Australian captain. "Come off it Don," he said, "this isn't the way to play cricket!"

"Well, you're the great batsman, Denis," Don replied, "it's up to you to show us how to play shots. I'm just trying to win the match!"

It struck me as quite amusing that two such great players were having a go at each other out in the middle during a Test. For my part, my stay at the wicket was, and is still, the slowest nought in Test cricket. We managed to save the match.

In 1948, The Don captained the most successful team to tour England. It was the final Test of the series, and his last, played at The Oval. Rain had played havoc with the ground, and when Norman Yardley won the toss and elected to bat, we were in dire trouble. Only Len Hutton made any contribution, and he was out, caught down the leg side by the man I regard as the greatest wicket-keeper of them all, Don Tallon. We were bowled out for 51.

When The Don came in to bat, he wanted only two runs to end his illustrious career with a Test batting average of 101. But the odds were against him. The second ball he received from Eric Hollis was a googly. Don played it as a leg-spinner and the ball nipped back between bat and pad to take the centre stump. Yardley had greeted Don by leading us all in a hearty 'three cheers'. Could it have been that this had brought tears to Don's eyes? Was that why he was unable to pick Eric's wrong 'un?

It was on the same ground in 1953 that we broke the Australian stranglehold on the Ashes. We won the Fifth Test, the other four having been drawn. During our first innings, I was batting with Trevor Bailey and we were both going well. Alan Davidson had been fielding on the fine leg boundary to Ray Lindwall and at extra cover for Bill Johnston, but while chatting to the umpire he'd forgotten to move back to the fence for a new Lindwall over. When Ray bowled his first delivery just outside my leg stump, I thumped it to the onside, shouting "Come on, two," and set off like a rocket. Trevor, who saw the ball travelling straight to Davidson, immediately shouted "No!"

I was so surprised that I tried to turn and slipped 'base over apex'. Despite a full length dive, I failed to make my ground. It taught me a lesson. Always have a good look around to see where the fielders are.

Another episode which brings a smile to my face whenever I think about it was Jim Laker's fantastic spell at Old Trafford in 1956 when he took those 19 wickets.

When he dismissed Keith Miller, caught at short leg off a lifter, I turned round to Tony Lock, that great competitor and Laker accomplice, to see him clapping his hands saying, "Well bowled, you bastard, give me the bloody ball!"

Standing there and watching Jim take wicket after wicket made Tony very frustrated. I also made him bowl faster and shorter. It does not pay to lose one's temper on the cricket field.

After Jim took his 19 wickets (Lock got the other) he drove off quietly back to London and stopped for dinner on the motorway. Everyone in the restaurant was watching the highlights on television and cheering each wicket. One guy turned to Jim and said, "What a performance—I'd give anything to meet that Laker".

Jim looked at him, gave a half smile and said, "Me too!"

by
Greg
Chappell

YOU CAN COUNT ON DOUG

Doug Walters was an integral part of Australian Ashes campaigns through the late 1960s and '70s and played some memorable innings in those encounters. As valuable as he was on the field much of his true value was off the field and behind the scenes, where his dry wit contributed so much to the wonderful team spirit of those years.

Much of Doug's card-playing skill was attributable to his iron-clad memory—a memory he used very well to add 'sting' to his humour. He would often file incidents away in his memory bank to be used at a later date. I was on the receiving end of one of these flashes of vintage Walters, spread over two tours of England, three years apart.

In 1972, we played the Third Test against England at Headingley on a pitch affected by a disease called 'fuserium', which killed the grass. It was uncanny that it only attacked a strip 22 yards by eight feet and the rest of the ground was perfectly healthy. Quite a coincidence, too, that England had selected two spinners for the match, but that's another story!

As we struggled on this dusty pitch, I felt attack was the best method of defence, but fell to a good catch from Derek Underwood's bowling as I attempted

149

to hit him over the infield.

I was frustrated and annoyed with myself as I walked into the dressing-room, which was deserted apart from Doug, who was putting on his pads for his turn at the crease. There was a clothes dryer next to my bag and as I passed it I slammed the door shut and said: "No f...ing justice in this game!" With that, I threw my bat into my bag.

Doug didn't say a word.

Three years later at the same ground, Doug walked in after being dismissed, whacked the same drying cabinet with his bat and said: "No f...ing justice in this game!" He sat down next to me, quite deadpan.

No one else in the room appreciated the humour, but I had a quiet chuckle to myself and thought: Touche! Another one to you, you little bugger!

Walters was a constant source of amusement and we never knew what to expect next. During a tour match at Nottingham one day, Rod Marsh remarked that it seemed a fair crowd and wondered out loud just how many people were there. Doug, fielding in the gully, said nothing.

As we changed ends a few overs later Doug sidled up to Rod and said: "Three thousand, two hundred and twenty-three!" Rod looked at him incredulously and said: "What?" As straight-faced as you like, Doug said: "No! Sorry! Three thousand, two hundred and twenty-five! Two more have just walked in!"

Between overs, he had counted everyone in the crowd!

'B-B-BRADMAN BILL'S' B-B-BROADSIDE

There are some who have suggested that my two seasons in England with the Somerset County Cricket Club taught me most of what I knew about the game. Certainly, it was a great experience and was a very important part of my cricket development as well as my all-round education. It was also of inestimable benefit in my first Ashes series because I had played against all the Englishmen on that tour in county cricket.

Our coach at Somerset in my two seasons there was Bill Andrews, who had bowled for the county in the 1930s. Bill's main claim to fame was having bowled Don Bradman in a tour match, although it must be pointed out that Bradman had scored more than 300 at the time. True to his light-hearted approach to life, Bill wrote a book on his rather mediocre career and titled it *The Hand That Bowled Bradman*. Bill, who had a bit of a stutter, was very good at self-promotion.

Although into his 60s, Bill kept himself in good shape and played the odd game and, as well as being the county's coach, he managed the second eleven.

Early in my first season, the first team had a few days off at a time when the seconds had a match against Hampshire at Southampton and Bill, realising I was on my own, invited me to travel with his team. I hadn't seen much of the country at that stage, so I jumped at the chance.

The second XI games were of two days duration and the Somerset side, which contained a few regular senior players, had the better of the first day. So much so that Hampshire had to follow-on and a Somerset victory appeared to be a mere formality. Confident of their chances, the Somerset boys began to celebrate their expected victory a night early and some were a little worse for the wear next morning. Bill, being early to bed, and a sound sleeper, missed most of the frivolities.

The cricket took a turn for the worse for Somerset that day and by lunch—thanks to some poor bowling and a couple of dropped catches—Hampshire looked like saving the match.

Bill, who was a social animal, had hardly seen a ball bowled as he had spent the morning perambulating around the ground regaling anyone who would listen with accounts of his first class wickets, including that of Bradman. When he returned to the pavilion he was mortified to find that Somerset had let the game slip. He checked with the scorer to find out what had gone wrong.

As the main offenders were the first XI players, he called the team together for a dressing down. Knowing he hadn't seen a ball bowled, I stayed close at hand to hear what he had to say. Being of the old school, Bill believed young players should be seen and not heard so I stayed out of the way as he addressed the culprits in his stuttering manner.

To one of our opening bowlers he said: "B-B-Burgess, that was s-s-some of the w-w-worst fast b-b-bowling I have ever seen!"

To our main spinner, "C-C-Clarkson, for an experienced off-s-s-spinner your line and l-l-length was atrocious!" And to the poor unfortunate who had dropped a couple of difficult catches: "B-B-Barnwell, I can't believe you d-d-dropped those c-c-catches!"

For fear of laughing out loud, I started to move away, but Bill turned on me and roared: "And as for you Ch-Ch-Chappell, as an overseas p-p-player you should be b-b-bloody well ashamed of yourself!"

"But Bill," I said, "I'm not even playing in the game".

Bill was not going to let logic interfere with his rage. "D-d-don't argue with m-m-me and get out of my b-b-bloody sight," he said as he stormed out of the dressing-room.

by
Ian
Wooldridge

PROTECTING THE GUILTY

It is with profound regret that I have to declare that practically every funny story I know about English or Australian cricketers is unprintable. I jotted down a dozen the other night but in the cold light of dawn expunged them on the grounds of discretion, libel or the fear of physical retribution.

So relax, chaps, wherever you are (which I hope, by now, is back in your own bedroom in a tolerably sober condition). This piece will be the soul of tact with absolutely no references to Freddie Trueman instructing a distinguished diplomat of darkish hue to pass the salt Gunga Din or why the winsome daughters of the Duke of Norfolk—whom he brought on tour to Australia when he was manager of the 1962–63 England team—became fondly known as the Norfolk Broads.

No, there will be none of that malarky here though, it would, of course, be remiss of me not to pay passing tribute to the splendid English national hero who, back in the days when the teams travelled from London to Fremantle by boat, actually rattled up a century before they even arrived in Australia.

Alas, this monumental achievement is to be found nowhere in the pages of Wisden.

Now, I fear, they only drink beer, the gold-medal

performances, as I understand it, being a mere 54 cans on a direct flight from Sydney to London. The result of this timid self-restraint was that Australia proceeded to give England one of the worst shellackings they have suffered this century.

It was not ever thus. My introduction to Australian humour came literally within minutes of landing at Fremantle as a war correspondent attached to the abovementioned Duke of Norfolk's raiding party. We had travelled from Aden on the SS Canberra, a convivial vessel, whose only drawback was that it was also carrying one Gordon Pirie, a British 5000-metres athlete. Somehow Mr. Pirie managed to ingratiate himself with the English cricket team who, in a moment of madness, suggested that between their sessions of deck quoits and bridge he may care to supervise their brief PT exercises so that they might arrive in Australia bearing some spurious semblance of fitness.

Pirie, whose propensity for making a quick buck was legendary to everyone in the world apart from the English cricket team, instantly accepted on the strict understanding that his Olympian principles debarred him from accepting anything so vulgar as fiscal remuneration. The lads liked that and constantly invited him to join them socially.

They were somewhat surprised, however, on driving in from Fremantle docks to their Perth hotel, to be confronted by alarming newspaper posters proclaiming: "England Cricketers on Drink Charge". Those brave enough to buy the papers then discovered Mr. Pirie's secondary talent, which was for maverick freelance journalism. No sooner had the Canberra docked than he was on the telephone to Western Australia's most prominent newspaper, selling them the exclusive information that, from what he had observed at close quarters, Australia was about to entertain a bunch of so-called professional sportsmen whose drinking routine would have made the founder of Alcoholics Anonymous blanch. In fact, the series was drawn and Gordon Pirie had the good sense to breeze on straight through to New Zealand.

For me, that initial visit was the beginning of a life-long affection for hanging around Australia but, before you begin to purr with pleasure, I should warn you that not every Pom reacts with quite the same warmth. On an earlier tour the legendary Beau Vincent, a predecessor of the incomparable John Woodcock, as cricket correspondent of the London *Times*, disembarked at Fremantle, sniffed the air, slumped into a corner chair in the bar of the now demolished Adelphi Hotel in Perth and for three days moodily reviewed the situation.

His conclusion was that he couldn't stand the place. He returned forthwith to Britain thus becoming, as far as I can ascertain, the only sportswriter in history to get out on a six-month 35,000–mile assignment and never write a word.

I greatly regret that such bumbling eccentricity is diminishing. Character more recently has been replaced by a nebulous quality known as charisma, which as often as not is a synonym for oafish behaviour bereft of even black humour.

Much preferable were the circumstances surrounding England's extraordinary decision in the early 1960s to recall to its expeditionary force to Australia one David Sheppard, who had last played for his country fully five years earlier and then headed off to take Holy Orders and attempt to save the souls of the criminal

FLAMIN' POMS — THEY'LL STOP AT NOTHING TO WIN THE ASHES... !

classes in London's East End. It was one of the more bizarre decisions in the history of cricket and became still more strange when the then chairman of the England selectors, Walter Robins, phoned Sheppard's Mission Control down in Cockneyland and left a message for Sheppard to phone him at Lord's Cricket

Ground the instant he returned from his latest errand of mercy.

As it happened Sheppard had for some weeks been pestered by a parishioner called Robins, whose sudden return to religious conviction may not have been unassociated with an inconvenient charge of causing grievous bodily harm or even attempted murder. In the circumstances, even Sheppard believed it would be preferable to allow justice to take its normal course and he tossed the message aside. Three days later he received a furious phone call from Walter Robins demanding to know whether he wanted to tour Australia or not.

Sheppard, absolutely flabbergasted, said he did. He proceeded to drop catches all over Australia but, after registering a duck in the first innings in Melbourne, scored a resolute 113 in the second to set up a seven-wicket victory for England in the Second Test. He returned to his native shores to become Bishop of Liverpool, which he still is, and earn himself the sobriquet in political circles of The Turbulent Priest. Never mind that, in his heyday he was one hell of a player.

To my dismay, cricket is much better organised these days. Players train, attend boring press conferences, make accomplished speeches at the openings of garages and supermarkets and comfort themselves, when it suits them, with a kind of dignity which suggests they think there may be some kind of lucrative career out there somewhere after playing Ashes cricket. Ashes cricket, of course, is the apotheosis and those of us who have never had the talent or chance dearly wish that those who now do would recognise that it is also a stage for high humour.

by
Colin
Cowdrey

G'DAY, SAID 'THOMMO'

At first mention, humour in the Ashes sounds a contradiction in terms, rather like chalk and cheese or, more appetisingly, hot chocolate sauce poured over vanilla ice cream. Indeed, a lot of people must find it difficult to associate levity with a game of cricket between the traditional protagonists, England and Australia. Yet cricket at any level—even Ashes level— has always produced its comedians and its comedy. Hopefully, it always will.

The most unusual Ashes experience I had was in Perth during the Second Test match in December, 1974, after being flown to Australia as a replacement for an injured player. It was 20 years since I had first toured Australia. I had watched the First Test on television from England and had never met the now rising star, Jeff Thomson.

It was just one of those strange things that we still had not met by the time I had walked to the wicket, batting No. 3 on the first morning of the Test match. He gave me a torrid time before lunch and again in the first hour after lunch. It happened that I was at the non-striker's end when he bowled the last ball before the mid-afternoon drinks interval, at which point all the players moved away from us towards the drinks trolley.

Jeff and I walked several yards apart, unspeaking for a while. Then, quite simultaneously, our thoughts were as one: "Enemies we might be but we have never met and I had better say hello." We found ourselves walking towards each other, hands outstretched, somewhat embarrassed at the formalities.

"How do you do. I'm Colin Cowdrey."

"G'day, I'm Jeff Thomson."

It was a Livingstone and Stanley greeting, a nervous smile and not much else to say as we went our separate ways in search of a wet towel and a cold drink. I doubt whether it could have happened before and whenever we meet we enjoy a smile about it—not that I find much to smile about as I recall the apprehension of having to stand up to his bowling.

It was towards the end of that afternoon when I had battled myself towards 44 hard-earned if not very entertaining runs, that a little, old, very sun-tanned Australian, sitting in front of the scoreboard with no shirt but a pile of empty beer cans beside him, started to heckle me. Misreading my name on the big scoreboard through his alcoholic haze, a piercing yell of "Cowboy" kept bellowing out over the ground.

At the end of an over I walked a few yards in his direction and took my hat off to acknowledge him. This brought a huge cheer from the crowd but he won the next trick and delighted them by shouting: "Cowboy, I used to come here and watch your father play and he wasn't very good either."

It was on the first morning of my third-ever Test match, in Melbourne in January, 1955, that Keith Miller gave me my first glimmer of humour amid the battle for the Ashes. Len Hutton had elected to bat on what appeared to be a straightforward, good, hard pitch; but there turned out to be quite a lot of moisture under the surface.

Inevitably, Miller and Ray Lindwall were to exploit this from the start and we had a dreadful morning. Miller in particular was at the top of his form and those who were present will never forget his seven eight-ball overs which produced three wickets for five runs. I am not sure those figures quite reflected his mastery, or the times he beat the bat.

I came to the wicket after half an hour, batting No. 4, and ten minutes later Miller had Hutton caught behind. In came Denis Compton. Miller and Compton were very close friends, but the sight of the Englishman 22 yards away in a Test Match, in front of 70,000 people, had the big Australian tossing back his mane of dark hair and striving for the utmost. Miller had a glorious physique and, this day, had hit upon a lovely rhythm.

After bowling a couple of really nasty ones which had nipped back off the seam and which Denis had managed to negotiate in miraculous fashion, Miller bowled a ball which pitched middle and took a sudden left fork with a huge leap at the same time. You could feel the crowd jump off their seats as they roared their appreciation.

Feigning a severe schoolmasterly frown, Miller shouted down the wicket: "Compo, Compo, you never seem to get any better—don't you ever practise?" He then turned to me at the non-striking end: "It's amazing, young Colin. They keep picking this joker, Compton— I suppose for his looks—but I have been bowling him this same ball since 1946 and he still doesn't wake up to it!"

As the ball was returned to him on his walk back, he stopped and half turned: "Are you awake now Denis? I don't want you to accuse me of bowling before you are ready." After the next ball, which Denis played in the middle of the bat, Miller said: "I have found the answer now—it is a much better game for everyone if I aim at your bat."

All this caused great merriment to the ring of close fielders and Denis loved it too. Nevertheless, the battle continued to be fought at a fierce intensity and Miller had Compton out the following over off an unplayable lifting ball, caught off his glove in the gully by Neil Harvey.

It was in that same match in Melbourne that Yorkshireman Johnny Wardle had some fun. Without a doubt, he was the most skilful clown I have seen on a cricket field. Johnny was able to balance it up well and he was scrupulously careful only to produce the funnies when there was little risk of them being considered an unsporting diversion. He knew, too, when not to do something which would have appeared out of place in the context of the match.

There was something about his craggy face, bent nose, chunky figure and brisk movements which had people warming to him before he did anything at all. When a game nosedived into a dull spell, he could be in his element and, for this alone, he was an invaluable member of a touring team.

After tea on one of the days of the MCG Test, the crowd in the beer corner became rather boisterous and started to barrack, throwing a few empty tins on to the field, quite near to where Johnny was fielding. Quick as a flash he waved, as if to thank them, for it had been a very hot day. He picked up two of the tins and went through the motions of emptying their contents. Immediately the large section of the crowd in that double-decker stand were on his side and even more so when, at the end of the over, he started to stagger around as if the beer was going to his head. Having got them into the palm of his hand he had them roaring with one of his major tricks.

Standing at cover point, he bent down to field a very hard slash, took it cleanly in his strong left hand—

for he was a brilliant fielder—and, timing it with precision, pretended the ball had gone through his legs. He turned in abjectly embarrassed fashion to chase off to the boundary after the non-existent ball.

There was an enormous shout of excitement from the crowd and the batsmen set off running, for nobody but Johnny had appreciated that he had the ball in his hand. After six or seven strides he put on the brakes, turned and threw the ball in to Godfrey Evans. There was a sudden shocked silence.

The crowd sensed the danger of an Australian batsman being run out. The batsmen, for their part, had to hustle. It was going to be tight.

But Evans, who had been through all this before, knew how to handle it. As the ball came in over the top of the stumps, he backed off four or five yards, took it cleanly and dived forward, making sure he was a long way short of taking the bails off.

The crowd took it all in very quickly and the silence turned to an eruption of noise and appreciation for Wardle's brilliant trickery and Godfrey Evans's sportsmanship.

These are the lovely moments which can only be occasional but are unforgettable and make a Test match day. Heaven knows what would have happened if the throw had hit the stumps!

If Wardle was the clown, Godfrey Evans was the star turn for producing continuous enthusiasm, bubble and good fun whenever he was on a cricket field. He was meticulously fair and careful not to put off the players if they wanted to be deadly serious. But if they gave any indication that they enjoyed a light-hearted touch or two, he was always coming up with something in a host of little ways. They may sound somewhat ordinary when described in writing, but they provided a lifeline of amusement at the time, lowered the temperature and helped the long hot day along no end.

There was a time in cricket when umpires were expected to inspect the ball every few overs. It came about because it had become 'trendy' for bowlers to complain about the seam lifting. At the end of one over, Evans found the ball in his hand and threw it to the umpire, Harry Baldwin. "There you are Harry," he said, "You'd better have a look at it".

Harry caught the ball and put it on the ground while he bent down a few yards behind the stumps to adjust one of the batsman's pads. Godfrey picked up the ball and gave it to Jim Laker at the same time nodding towards Harry. Laker cleverly placed it at the foot of the middle stump on the batsman's side at the bowler's end. The players took up their positions and, after a long pause, the bowler asked for the ball. No one seemed to know where it was. It was a mystery. Godfrey then imposed himself on the scene and shouted in mock annoyance, "Wake up Harry! I've just given it to you. The ball's in your pocket!"

Remembering that Godfrey had indeed given him the ball, Harry buried his hands in his pockets and found a spare new ball—but not the ball we had been using. Now he was really in a flap. Godfrey allowed the embarrassment to continue a few more seconds and then shouted: "Why have you hidden it by the stumps Harry? Come on, we haven't time to waste—we want to win the game!"

Everyone fell about and Harry enjoyed the joke tremendously. He enjoyed it even more when he smiled and gave Godfrey Evans out leg before the next time he was standing in a Kent match. Godfrey bought him a bottle of champagne that evening.

A mental picture I always carry with me is the one of the late Jimmy Burke, a very fine opening batsman for Australia in the 1950s and himself quite a comedian. Jim was cruising back for a second run and thought he had it well in hand. He kept his eye on Godfrey as a guide to the arrival time of the throw in. Sensing that Jimmy was taking it for granted that he would get home, Godfrey moved early and rushed through the motions of collecting the ball and taking off the bails. Burke was thunderstruck for a moment, then dived full length to save himself. "That was tight, Jimmy," said Godfrey. "You're getting old."

Jimmy spent an age dusting himself down and it was Colin McDonald, his batting partner, who eventually told him there had been a misfield, he had never been in danger and the ball wasn't in Godfrey's gloves when the bails were removed. When the message got through, Jimmy laughed aloud, shook his head and said: "You win, Godfrey—but you'll be getting the laundry bill!"

Yes, we had a lot of laughs during the very serious business of playing for the Ashes. I hope they still have as many today.

C'MON AUSSIE C'MON

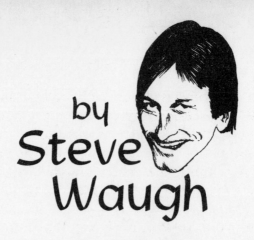

by
Steve
Waugh

SNAKEBITE!

We had just pulled off what many people thought impossible—we had bowled England out in 50 overs on a batsman's paradise on the last day of the First Test at Headingley, traditionally Australia's graveyard ground.

Needless to say the celebrations began as soon as we were greeted in our dressing-room by our fellow players and management. It wasn't long before everyone was drenched in champagne and beer, with the sounds of Cold Chisel blaring from the team music machine. There was only one very important event the team had to perform—the team song, led by D. Boon, who positioned himself on the dressing-room table and led all the tour party into song, making everyone feel proud to be an Australian and part of a team which would, hopefully, even though there were still five Tests to go, bring home the Ashes.

The festivities in the room ended some considerable time later with most of the boys exhibiting the inner and outer glow of satisfaction which comes from gently celebrating a job well done.

Due to the team's very tight schedule we were then all required to board the team coach for a two-hour trip to Manchester, with the next day's game against

Lancashire the furthest thing from anyone's mind! We had a few more celebratory drinks on the bus, though things were much quieter now, except for Merv molesting most of the passengers, and the occasional team song. It was a break between the dressing-room festivities and our eventual destination, the Copthorne Hotel in Manchester.

The bus pulled into this pit stop at around 9 p.m. and soon afterwards the lads gathered at Pier 6, which was to be our local watering hole whenever the team was in Manchester. 'Boonie' (David Boon) and 'Moods' (Tom Moody) carefully examined the cocktail list and announced, as men of experience, they could recommend both the Zambuccas and the Snake Bites.

Meantime, 'Heals' (Ian Healy) had begun his imitations of Tim May's, Merv Hughes' and Terry Alderman's bowling styles, with the run-ups beginning outside the pub doors and continuing right past the bar in front of an interested but rather bemused Pommie crowd. All good things finally come to an end and the celebrations finished at about a quarter to, or was it a quarter past! Anyway a great time was had by all.

Next morning it was back to business as the team arrived at Old Trafford to play against a Lancashire side which included Wasim Akram and Patrick Patterson, two of the world's fastest bowlers. As stand-in captain, Geoff Marsh walked out to the centre square to toss. It looked alarmingly like a quick bowlers' pitch and all the batsmen among the previous night's party-goers prayed the coin would land kindly for our captain, and as luck would have it we ended up fielding first, to the intense delight of the team.

It wasn't long before the match turned into a comedy of errors when, in the fourth over of the morning, Boon, fielding at short-leg, spilled the easiest chance in the history of the game. The Lancashire opening bat failed to cope with a rising delivery from Greg Campbell and popped the ball gently into the air where 'Boonie', three yards away, reacted like a startled cat. Unfortunately he lost his balance, slipped forward, and his helmet blocked his sight of the ball which lobbed on to his forearm. His efforts to retrieve the situation only had him ending up in a crumpled mess on the ground with the ball sitting on the turf close by.

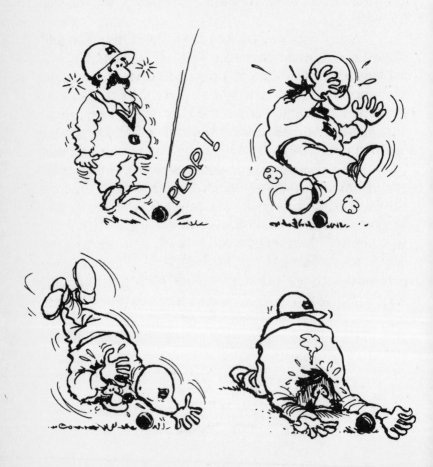

The whole team, the spectators and, not least, the lucky batsman, were stunned and it wasn't until 'Boonie' gathered himself together and stood up laughing that the fielding side, other than perhaps Greg Campbell, broke into fits of laughter.

The match restarted but the laughter was contagious every time we looked at 'Boonie', now crouching and grim-faced. The slips cordon was unable to stop, including captain Marsh who, while shedding tears of laughter, spilled another straightforward chance at first slip soon afterwards, claiming he couldn't see the ball because of tears.

Everyone now thought the fun was over, but it wasn't to be as two overs later the Lancashire batsmen had an appalling misunderstanding in midwicket, creating a chance for a run out which Tom Moody tried to perform by throwing down the stumps at the bowler's end. His throw missed with the still embarrassed Boon backing up. Perhaps 'backing up' is too strong a phrase, because he slipped once again and went down like a ton of bricks, his helmeted head crashing into the turf, resulting in four overthrows, much to the annoyance of Greg Campbell who once again was the bowler.

When the first session came to an end we had put down seven chances but by hell we'd provided great entertainment not just for the local crowd but for each other on the field!

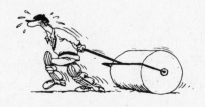

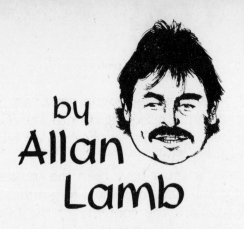

by
Allan
Lamb

SLEDGING, YOU BEAUTY!

When it comes to sledging at cricket the Aussies are the experts. No one, but no one, gives the backchat as smartly as the men in those baggy green caps. Mind you, the Aussies ought not start thinking they invented sledging.

That great Englishman W. G. Grace knew a bit about getting everyone going from umpires to opponents to match promoters. There's the lovely tale about our Amazing Doctor replacing a dislodged bail almost before the bowler had time to get excited.

As he did so he delivered the famous line, "Look my good man, the crowds have come here to see me bat, not you bowl".

On another occasion, after he had succeeded in gaining another dubious leg before decision, he confided to the despondent, outgoing batsman, "You weren't out, you know," thus liberally rubbing salt into the poor chap's wound.

Of course it's not just the boys in the baggy green who have taken up where the Good Doctor left off; those Aussie spectators are sharp, too. For sheer originality you would be hard pressed to beat the day a piglet stopped play during the Brisbane Test of the 1987–88 season.

A group of enterprising young veterinary students smuggled the tranquilised piglet into the 'Gabba by hiding him inside an Esky, every Aussie's refrigerated portable drinks' cabinet.

Those students must have been the smoothest fast talkers in Queensland, because the ground stewards had asked to check the contents of the Esky. They raised an eyebrow or two at the sight of the stunned piglet—with an apple stuck in its mouth, do you mind!—But they were led to believe it was a suckling pig barbecue-bound.

When the piglet emerged from its comatose state the timing was perfect. Ian Botham, England's all-rounder, was at the wicket.

On one side of the piglet was scrawled 'Beefy' and on the other 'Eddie', none too subtle references to the porky waistlines of Ian, our star all-rounder, and Hemmings, our offspinner. And the piglet's tail had been decorated with a Union Jack. Now that's what I call a sledge.

And, of course, it led to the now famous sledge by our opening batsman, Graeme 'Foxy' Fowler, on Eddie as they drove back to the hotel at the end of the day. Eddie was at the wheel, 'Foxy' in the back and obviously keen to make greater haste. "Any chance of going a bit quicker and putting your trotter on the gas?" he asked Eddie.

One of my earliest encounters with Australians giving me a send-off was in the Perth Test in the 1982–83 season. Dennis Lillee was bowling and Rod Marsh was wicket-keeping and I got the full blast of their displeasure when I stayed at the crease after they thought I was caught behind.

Dennis's appeal was bellowed loudly enough to have been heard way off in Fremantle, but I tell you it was mild compared to the bellow of rage he aimed in my direction when the umpire begged to differ.

As often happens in those circumstances I went on to get a few runs before I was eventually caught in the slips. Rod Marsh gave me a personal escort for quite a few yards, at the same time ordering me to stay on course and I'd find the dressing sheds.

Later over a few beers with DK and Marshy I stitched them up by explaining I was merely complying with that great old Australian cricketing tradition: don't walk, even if you think the ball has taken a chunk of wood out of your bat!

David Hookes once hit Tony Greig with what must be close to the perfect sledge. When Hookes was still being described by the media as 'youthful'—in the Centenary Test in Melbourne in 1977, in fact—'Greigy' let him have a broadside of uncomplimentary remarks.

'Greigy's' comments so concentrated Hookes' mind that he cracked the England captain for five consecutive boundaries.

Some might say a case of the wrong words at the wrong time. How then would you assess Ian Botham's words of encouragement to me in that 1982–83 series when Dennis Lillee and Rodney Hogg were making me look like an out-of-form village cricketer one Test?

In came the mighty 'Both' with his bat-swinging, loosening-up exercises. I watched him coming towards the middle looking like one of King Richard's knights getting the feel of his broadsword on his way to the Battles of the Crusades.

He would have seen my plight. I wondered what sound technical advice, what sort of encouragement he would offer. He strode to my end of the pitch and said, "They must be staging the Miss World Contest at the MCG today, 'Lambie'; I've never seen so many good looking women at a cricket match. You're disappointing them, so start batting properly!"

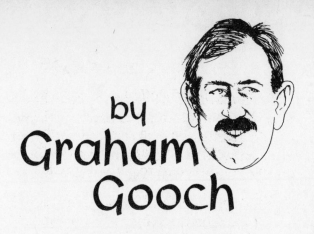

by Graham Gooch

UNLIKELY ALLIES

Not too many of England's batsmen had anything nice to say about Dennis Lillee and Jeff Thomson in the mid-1970s—but they did me a big favour and helped me into the Test arena in 1975. Not that I lasted too long that time, but without them I probably would have waited several more seasons for my England debut.

I got my chance at the tender age of 21, and after less than a season of county cricket with Essex, because Mike Denness's side had been destroyed on their 1974-75 tour of Australia. 'Thommo' and Lillee had wreaked havoc among England's batsmen and, predictably, the British media clamoured for some new and young blood. Ian Chappell's side arrived in England a few months later and made the first—and, so far, the best—World Cup Final before narrowly losing out to the West Indies. The four England Tests were to follow.

The MCC match against the tourists just before the First Test was being used by the selectors as a sort of trial. I'd hit form at the right time, was picked and earned my Test place with 75 against the Australians at Lord's.

Despite the problems of the previous winter, I was the only new batsman in the line-up, although Kent's

Bob Woolmer was made 12th man. Being such a new boy, I was pretty nervous at breakfast on the morning of the Test. I knew very few of the England officials and several of my team mates were strangers as well.

A face I did recognise was Sir Leonard Hutton, one of the all-time great batsmen and now an England selector. Not unnaturally, I felt my presence in the Test side was largely attributable to his assessment of my potential. But I felt I'd just been bowled with a full toss when he asked me: "Have you ever played against Australia before?" I hesitated. "Well, yes," I said, "I assumed you'd picked me to play for MCC against them last week!"

I never really resolved that one. Nor did I make much of an impact on the match. It was certainly a memorable occasion—not least for my nightmare start to Test cricket with an eight-ball 'pair'. Mike Denness became the first England captain to win the toss and elect to field in an Edgbaston Test. Four days later, he became the first England captain to lose an Edgbaston Test. England had a new captain for the Second Test at Lord's. Nothing humdrum about my introduction to Test cricket.

After the Australians had scored 359—with Rick McCosker, Ian Chappell, Ross Edwards and Rod Marsh all passing 50—we batted for just one over before the heavens opened. Wickets were uncovered then and Lillee, Thomson and Max Walker had a field day as they ran amok on a rain-affected pitch to destroy us twice, for 101 and 175.

The Test also went into the record books because of the number of umpires used—four! Arthur Fagg and Dickie Bird started the proceedings, but Dickie injured his back on the third day. Fortunately, Alan Oakman, a former Test player and first class umpire, was at the ground and he took over after tea. Tom Spencer was sent for and deputised on the fourth day.

But it was Australian wicket-keeper Rodney Marsh who made the most lasting impression on me . . . and the Edgbaston dressing-room. Play was held up while the ball was changed when the tourists were batting. There was no suitable replacement so we had to hang around for ten minutes while one was bashed about in the nets. You can imagine that Rod was not best pleased when he was caught by Keith Fletcher off the first ball back. It happens time and time again. Just a little interruption can upset a batsman's concentration.

Marsh stormed off in a fury. Now, as cricket lovers know, there's a lot of glass in the dressing-room area at Edgbaston and, really, we were not surprised when we heard an enormous crash a few seconds after Marsh had disappeared from view. Apparently, in his frustration, his bat had slipped out of hands and had, unluckily, found its way through a glass door.

Rod was one of the unforgettable characters of Australian cricket. Another, for me, was Scott Ledger. Maybe not as well known, but he made quite an impression on Mike Brearley's England tourists in 1978–79.

We were playing at Bundaberg and Ledger was the Queensland Country XI's opening bat. We thought we'd seen the last of him when he flashed at John Lever and edged a big snick to our 'keeper. But Ledger remained unmoved—as did the umpire's finger. Not surprisingly, a few words were exchanged, but Ledger was unrepentent. It was in the true tradition of Australian batsmen, as described by South African

Barry Richards: "The only time an Aussie walks is when his car runs out of petrol!"

Lever was by now fired up and dug in a good bouncer. Ledger, again in true Australian tradition, accepted the challenge and went to hook. He missed, the side of his head was split open and there was blood everywhere. "We won't see him again," were our thoughts as he was helped off and taken to the local hospital. But we had misjudged our man as seriously as he had misjudged Lever's bouncer.

By mid-afternoon he was back, head bandaged and ready to re-enter the fray. And when he did, another bouncer was delivered to see if he'd learned his lesson. He had, because he decided discretion was the better part of valour and moved to get out of the way.

Unfortunately, that earlier blow on the head had slowed down his reactions as he took evasive action. The ball thudded into the other side of his head this time, but the results were the same—split head, more blood, helped off and despatched to the local hospital.

Amazingly, Ledger returned to the ground that evening. We thought he was trying for third time lucky, but this time our resilient batsman was only heading for the bar, where he received a well-deserved hero's welcome from the locals and the well-earned respect of the England touring party.

C'MON AUSSIE C'MON

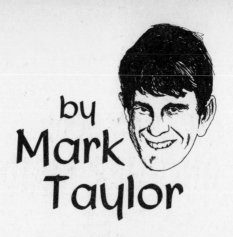

by
Mark
Taylor

OUT OF BOUNDS

Female streaking came back into vogue during the '89 Ashes tour. It began with a lovely lady performing cartwheels in front of the Lord's pavilion during the final one-day game against England and ended with another topless talking with Ian Botham and Allan Border in the middle of Old Trafford during the Fourth Test.

However, the one that really caught my eye and landed me in the most trouble was the quick-sprinting brunette at Headingley on the final day's play of the First Test.

Day five of the match proved to be one of the most important day's play of the series and I think the streaker may have assisted us to a victory. At the time of her maiden dash, our foes were five wickets down and the pressure was really on. That now-famous dash may have relaxed us all to the extent that it brought about the enemy's downfall!

It wasn't so much the streaker herself who landed me in trouble, rather it was the photo of her that captured me in the background with a grin from ear to ear. Sporting a rather satisfied look on my face didn't help my cause and, in fact, brought about a torrid time for me.

The photo was used in many English tabloids the following morning, including the local *Bury Times*. Now it just so happened I had been given the following game off by the tour selectors and I decided to head for Bury where I had played League cricket the previous season. However, I wasn't returning to Bury to see some old friends, but rather to visit my wife who had flown in from Australia two days previously. When I finally arrived I expected to be greeted with a warmth and fervour befitting a couple who had been parted for six weeks. Instead I had to do a neat sidestep to dodge the latest edition of the *Bury Times* and was left with a lot of quick explaining to do to my better half concerning camera angles, pressure of the game and other important matters!

Being as keen on my golf as I am on cricket, I enjoyed the many rounds we played before and on the rest days of the Test matches. One round played at Mere Golf Club, Manchester, before the Fourth Test will always remain in my memory, thanks to David Boon.

During this particular round, Allan Border and I were teamed against Geoff Marsh and David Boon. It just so happened that coming to the 16th hole the match was all-square and, although the stakes weren't high, there was plenty of pride up for grabs.

AB, myself and 'Swamp' had already teed off and 'Babs' was preparing for his assault. The 16th hole is a long par-4 which dog-legged sharply to the left. If you decide to use a one wood you must hit the ball as close to the pines on the left as possible to avoid the out-of-bounds area on the right.

'Babs' decided to use the driver and hit a screamer down the left, very close to the trees. Being his opponent for the day meant I stood behind him and urged the ball into the trees and, sure enough, the ball hit the very edge of the last tree and dropped to the base. 'Babs' swung around, called me every possible name and threatened to do all sorts of ugly things to me with the one wood. He did, fortunately for me, cool down and we slowly made our way down the fairway.

On reaching the ball, 'Babs' found it positioned in such a way that he could only hit it by turning the club around and swinging left-handed, which he did. To everyone's surprise—not least his own—he made superb contact with the ball, hitting it so squarely that, rather than into the perfect position he had envisaged, it hurtled right across the fairway and out-of-bounds on the other side.

I'm afraid this was the straw which broke the camel's back and after abusing me once again, he disgustedly threw the eight iron straight up in the air.

The club flew into the branches of the tree under which he was standing and, like a fun ball it bounded from limb to limb. When the eight iron finally returned to the ground it had a rather pronounced bend in the middle of the shaft. Now this would not have been a major problem had David owned the clubs. However, they were supplied to the team and at the end of the tour were to be returned or else bought for £200 a set.

As you might imagine, 'Babs' spent the remainder of the 16th hole straightening out the eight iron as he had no intention of purchasing the set.

At the end of the tour most of the clubs were bought by the members of the press who followed the team on tour. One unlucky soul, whose handicap has ballooned in recent times, still has trouble figuring out why his eight iron is constantly finishing in the front bunker!

by Dean Jones

A BIT OVER THE FENCE, TIM!

Euphoria for me was always going to be playing a part in the reclaiming of the Ashes. I wasn't too fussy about which part I played as long as the mission was accomplished. Twelfth man would have been fine; baggage man would have done. To have actually been actively involved in the glorious 1989 campaign in England is the high point of my career and if I'm still saying that the day I retire, I won't be disappointed at all. But what a shame, personally, that the Terrible Tims were also on that tour.

Tim May and Tim Zoehrer were good mates of mine and, despite what they did to me, still are. I'm still half expecting a letter from Mr. Z containing the equivalent of 600 English pounds. The covering note will probably say something like: "I can't accept it. I couldn't do it to you."

Team mates tell you a lot of secrets in the course of a long tour, and over a few beers one night, the other Tim (that's May) confided that he'd never hit a six. Not in a social, club, first class or Test match. Not even in his backyard cricketing days.

Armed with this information, I immediately devised a sure-fire, couldn't-miss way to make a quid. I let it be known that I was prepared to bet 50/1 against

Timothy Ernest May hitting a six on that tour.

Word got around—but, unfortunately, so did Tim's track record. There were no takers, not even when, in true leviathan bookmaker tradition, I lengthened the odds to 60/1. For three months I sat back waiting for suckers who didn't arrive. Then, on August 16—I remember the date very well—up bobbed Tim Zoehrer. He'd just made a huge killing with Ladbrokes on Mark Calcavecchia's victory in the British Open golf championship and he was dead keen to press his luck. "I want to back Tim May to hit a six," he said. "Is the offer still open?"

"Sure," I replied. "For any amount. How much do you want?" Tim ostentatiously flipped through a huge bundle of notes he produced from his blazer pocket and said 600 pounds to 10 would do him very nicely, thank you.

We were playing Kent at Canterbury and were sent in to bat on a very green pitch. Despite conditions better suited to bowling, we did fairly well, David Boon making 80-odd and yours truly 120. One of Kent's best bowlers was a left-arm orthodox spinner named Kelleher, and he just happened to have the ball when Tim May came to the crease.

The Australian party were on the balcony urging Tim to have a go at this spinner and hit him out of the ground. And of course, the loudest urging was being done by a fellow named Zoehrer. I was still feeling very confident about my bet, the more so because Tim (May, I mean) hadn't bothered to back himself. Obviously, I thought, he still thought himself incapable of a six.

Tim played the first two balls from Kelleher very defensively, but the coaxing from our balcony obviously got to him because he went for a real windy woof on the third delivery. He skied it and I watched with a great deal of satisfaction as a fieldsman got under it, no more than 20 yards from the bat. To my utter disbelief, he dropped a real dolly of a catch.

A certain Australian player among us roundly abused the unfortunate Kent chap for a disgraceful piece of fielding. Indeed, the words were such that they cannot be reproduced here.

I was more confident than ever of having Tim Zoehrer's 10 pounds in my pocket at tour's end. Tim May, I thought, was the type of person who would learn from his recklessness and henceforth—in this particular innings, anyway—play conservatively and along the ground.

Oh, how I misjudged him! The next ball was spun up—and swept with an elegance which would have done justice to Tom Moody. It was a magnificent sweep and it sailed long and high into the members' car park! One of the sweetest sixes I had ever seen. It was certainly the costliest.

Tim May's body language told the full story of his delight and the Australian laughter on the balcony seemed to go on for hours. And Tim Zoehrer laughed loudest and longest.

The moral of the story, of course, is never ever bet on cricket. I don't know who coined the words about the glorious uncertainties of cricket, but whoever it was has my total respect.

C'MON AUSSIE C'MON

189

A BEER BY ANY OTHER NAME

Castlemaine XXXX was the official sponsor of the Australian touring team and part of the deal required rostered players to visit pubs and try to persuade the locals to switch from their favourite beer to XXXX. Old beer-drinking habits die hard wherever you are, so it was certainly no pushover.

I was rostered with Merv Hughes at one particular pub promotion and although the locals weren't exactly queuing up to pledge new-found allegiance to our brew, the night was going very well. Merv and I were explaining—with actions and a great deal of pleasure—the best way to quaff an Aussie beer.

There was quite a debate on which beer—XXXX or Carling Black Label, the local product—was the better and the discussion got quite animated. Merv adopted his own sales pitch, which involved lifting a can of XXXX to his mouth, taking a healthy draught from it and saying: "This beer is the best beer in the world!" After several of these performances, the locals decided it was time to bring the big Australian fast bowler undone.

With a wink to me, but unbeknown to Merv, they filled an empty XXXX can with Carling, which is darker and stronger than XXXX and very, very distinguishable. Merv took the can, drank deeply of it, wiped his moustache, smacked his lips and quoted his now-famous quote: "This beer is the best beer in the world!"

The locals had done Merv quite roundly and they loved it. But neither they nor I had the heart to tell him there was something terribly wrong with his taste buds.

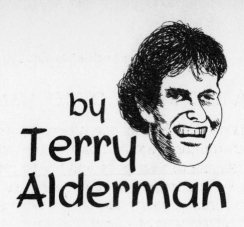

by
Terry
Alderman

DEREK FROM CAIRNS

Headingley cricket ground is one of the more famous venues in the cricket world. The scene of Bradman's 334 and 304 and the famous victory in 1938, it is also the disaster area of Australia's defeats in 1956 and 1961. It holds particularly bad memories for me. I will always be haunted by that nightmare Test—Australia vs England at Headingley in 1981 in which Ian Botham smashed two enormous sixes off my bowling as part of his incredible score of 149 and then Bob Willis took 8/43—thus giving victory to England and condemning me and the rest of the Austalian team to recurring nightmares and much soul searching. "How did Australia lose a Test match that really was theirs for the taking?"

It was therefore with mixed feelings of fear and desire for revenge that I approached the First Test of the 1989 Ashes tour at Headingley. Towards the end of the fourth day of play, with Allan Border desperate to obtain a 400-plus run lead to give Australia every chance of winning on the fifth day, umpires John Holder and David Shepherd decided to offer AB the option of stopping for bad light. He promptly declined as both he and Dean Jones were in fine form, hitting the ball to all parts of the ground and averaging about 10 runs per over.

Then, two overs later, much to AB's dismay, the umpires decided it was too wet to continue playing and called the players from the field with four overs still remaining in the day's play.

AB's face was a study of bubbling rage as he entered the dressing-room. Lamenting our loss of playing time, particularly at a time when both players were in peak form, but mindful of observing the umpires' decision, AB sat down and fixed his gaze on the telephone,

perhaps willing it to ring and hear the umpires say play would restart. No ring. No conversation either. Deathly quiet. AB, when he believes he is being 'dudded', has that effect on light-hearted, trivial conversation. You could have cut the air with a knife. Suddenly, like a fire alarm, the phone rang. Ian Healy, closest to it, picked it up, and, after several moments of nodding, but saying nothing, handed the phone to AB.

AB, still seething with fury, took the phone, hopeful it just might be the match referee giving the all-clear for further play and Healy had merely been trying to be polite. After a few seconds the furious look on our captain's face turned to one of amazement and then finally to a huge grin: "Sure, I'll tell them, bye."

He turned to the rest of us and said, grinning from ear to ear: "That was Derek from Cairns (Australia) and he said, 'What the f... is going on over there AB? Me and me mates have been sitting here all bloody night watching the telly and having a few beers and just when Australia was killing the Poms they stop play. You tell 'em AB, to stop f...ing around and get back on the bloody field!' "

Laughter broke out from all corners of the room as we realised with amazement that, from 10,000 miles away, Derek from Cairns was able to get through almost immediately and speak to the Australian captain. Not only did he have the correct phone number but he'd also managed to dial it, despite consuming quite a few beers, and *then* get through the red tape of the Test match office switchboard to our dressing-room!

Derek from Cairns will never know how timely his call was that day and what an ice-breaker it was— at the end of the game and a *win* to Australia, and after the usual toast, we all raised our glasses to Derek.

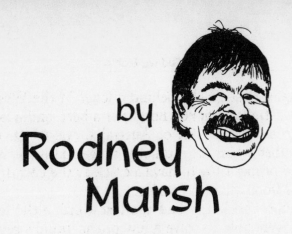

by Rodney Marsh

'CHAPPELLI'S' TOAST

Beating the Poms is one thing, thrashing them is really something else. So when I use the word 'triumph', an inadequate appraisal if ever there was one, to describe Allan Border's 1989 Ashes tour of England, you'll understand why I became a wicket-keeper, not a novelist.

It had been 55 years since an Australian team had won back the Ashes on English soil, quite a cause for celebration.

I lobbed in the Old Dart for the last two Tests, at Trent Bridge and The Oval, to do some work as a Nine Network commentator. Of course it was all over, Aussies three up, by then, the coveted Urn back where it belonged.

It did the old Marsh heart good to see the blokes I had played with in past years looking so completely content with life, and above all so tickled about their cricket.

I had my wife Roslyn with me and we reckoned the least we could do was to invite all the West Australian members of the touring party to dinner on the Saturday night of the Trent Bridge Test.

Travelling with Roslyn and me were Bob and Jenny Slade; Bob is manager of FAI Insurances in Perth, a company that's right behind cricket in the West, and also Australian cricket. Bob loves a beer, and a laugh.

Before we flew out of Australia, one of us, I can't remember which one, quietly suggested it might be a fit and proper time to have a crack at the beer drinking record from Perth to London.

Roslyn and Jenny had the last word, although Bob and I were able to solve a few of the world's problems between Perth and Hong Kong. Naturally Bob and Jenny were invited to the dinner with the WA boys.

The players who were free for dinner that evening included Geoff Marsh and his wife Michelle, Terry Alderman and his wife Jane, and Tom Moody. Also in the party was Geoff Marsh's brother Steve, and his wife.

There was one ring-in, Ian Chappell, a Croweater, a South Australian. The reason for this was that 'Chappelli' is a mate and was at a loose end.

The next day was a rest day in the Test, so I could hardly let him spend the night sitting in his hotel room by himself. And anyway I figured it would add to his education on life to get out with a group of we West Aussies.

Tom Moody didn't arrive until we were half way through our first pint. Tom noticed this and mentioned that he'd been in this same hotel for dinner a couple of nights before. "If you want a steady flow of drinks to the table my advice is to order the next when you're half way through the one in your hand," advised Tom.

Tom is only a youngster but I thought that suggestion showed great maturity; sure enough, just as we finished one pint another arrived. Bob and I were mightily impressed. Tom had his mind on other things.

Of course the main topic of dinner conversation was

cricket; it always is when cricketers and ex-cricketers get together.

The presence of 'Chappelli' was fortuitous because he has so much knowledge about the game and is always more than happy to pass it on to the current players if they are willing to listen.

Tom, and the other West Aussies don't get to talk to 'Chappelli' much so they were hanging on every word, and every story, every one of which reinforced the magic of an Australian cricket victory, especially the ones over England.

Even so, when my tough former captain leapt to his feet around midnight and began to launch into a very emotional victory toast to the team, it came as a real shock to me.

His toast to the young blokes, on behalf of a couple of old warriors (him and me), really left a lump in my throat. And as I looked around me I'd say a few young blokes felt the same as they appreciated the enormity of their achievements.

by Simon O'Donnell

A FLYING START

My best, and worst, memory of cricket in England concerns my first Test match for Australia in 1985.

I was one of the youngest and most inexperienced players on the 1985 Ashes tour of England and few people thought I would play any part in the Test matches. I hoped to use the tour to get the feel of international cricket and learn as much as possible.

This situation changed dramatically however when my form in the lead-up games was reasonably good and I was lucky enough to score an unbeaten century against MCC at Lord's. With other players experiencing moderate form, or becoming injured, I suddenly found myself in contention for a place in the team for the First Test match at Leeds.

I rang my parents at home in Deniliquin, in southern New South Wales, and explained I might be selected. They decided to fly over on the chance that I might be in. As they were unable to book a flight out of Australia until the day before the Test, it meant they arrived in England on the morning of the first day's play.

In a mad scramble they rushed off the plane at Heathrow and managed to catch a train to Leeds. From the station they took a bus to their hotel and from

there managed to jump straight into a taxi for the ground. My mother and father hurried into the Headingley Oval just as Australia lost their fifth wicket. I was next in.

Completely exhausted, yet thrilled to have made it in time, they settled down to watch my innings. I was out first ball. I cannot remember even seeing the ball as it left the bowler's hand. The scorebook read S. O'Donnell, lbw Botham, 0. Length of innings two minutes.

My parents had travelled for over 40 hours, with no sleep, to watch me bat, or almost bat, for two minutes. At least they were able to sleep peacefully throughout the rest of the day's play.

The second innings was not much better, although I did manage to entertain my parents for a little longer. When I went in to bat the spinners were operating from both ends and I was surrounded by bat-pad fielders. The ball was turning sharply and John Emburey was bowling very accurately. My feet felt like lumps of cement and I wondered how I was even going to lay bat on ball, let alone score. Wayne Phillips was batting well at the other end and between overs I walked down the pitch to seek his advice.

"I'm sorry 'Flippa', I'm not going too well at the moment. I've got no idea how I'm going to score."

His only reply was, "Don't worry about it. You're about to see the best century ever scored in Test cricket."

I was on nought for 43 minutes before I managed to snick one past leg slip to get off the mark. Wayne Phillips made a magnificent 91, we put on 80 of which I was able to contribute 24 and I gained some wonderful experience. I also learned the importance of confidence and my parents enjoyed some good batting, certainly better than the first innings.

A NOT SO EXPERT COMMENTATOR

I was not selected for the 1989 Ashes tour, but found myself in England playing local cricket and commentating on the Tests for Channel Nine. Commentating was a marvellous experience for me. I learned a great deal listening to and watching the techniques of former players like Richie Benaud, Ian Chappell and Rod Marsh.

At first I was terribly nervous appearing as an 'expert' next to men who had played and watched cricket for so many years. I was terrified of making a comment that was not appropriate or a prediction which would turn out to be totally incorrect.

It was during the Third Test at Trent Bridge I saw a chance to impress the listeners and my fellow commentators.

Whilst Australia were batting I visited the dressing-rooms to say hello to some of the players. As I entered the Aussie rooms I noticed Allan Border and Dean Jones were sitting with their pads on ready to go in and bat. Normally only one batsman is padded up and Dean Jones was listed to bat next.

I asked 'Deano' why he and AB were both padded up. He explained that the two batsmen in at the moment were going well because they formed a left-hand, right-hand combination. Mark Taylor (a left-hand batsman) was batting with David Boon (a right-hander) and this was making it difficult for the bowlers to settle into a steady line and length.

If Taylor went, Border would go in as he was left-handed, and if Boon was dismissed, Jones would bat as he was right-handed.

Australia did not lose a wicket before it was again

my turn in the commentary box.

I was commentating with Richie Benaud and we were concentrating on the way the Australian batsmen were playing and the tactical situation for Allan Border. I said that I wouldn't be surprised if Taylor were to be dismissed, Allan Border would replace him and not Dean Jones who was listed on the scorecard to come in next, adding that this would make certain the Australians could keep going with the left-hand right-hand combination to keep the English bowlers off balance.

Sure enough, a few balls later, Taylor was dismissed and Border came in. In the commercial break Richie was suitably impressed by this series of events and predictions and said, "That was great Simon, great thinking".

"Thanks Richie," I replied, "I like to be a thinking man's cricketer."

If ever you notice that a prediction from one of the commentators has come true, think twice before believing he is an expert. He might just have had a little advance knowledge!

About the Authors

ALLAN BORDER: tough-as-teak Australian captain who won back the Ashes in England in 1989, an achievement denied to all other Down Under Coin-Tossers since 1934. Holds records for scoring runs and catching catches in Tests, too.

ROBIN SMITH: born in South Africa but bats for English County team Hampshire, and now England, for obvious reasons. Hits the ball with tremendous power and head-to-head battles with Merv Hughes were a highlight of the 1989 Ashes series.

RICHIE BENAUD: former Australian captain and great legspinning all-rounder. His 1958 team won the Ashes back from England. Now a commentator for the Nine Network and also the BBC in England.

GRAHAM McKENZIE: his magnificent physical build and rugged, curly-haired good looks earned him the nickname 'Garth' after the famous comic strip tough man. Great fast bowler and fighting batsman.

FRANK TYSON: swept onto the world scene in the 50s with pace like fire but such were the stresses placed on his body his career was shortened by constant injury. Bowled so fast the crowds called him 'Typhoon'.

TREVOR BAILEY: England all-rounder who loved nothing more than to fight a brave, rearguard action. Nicknamed 'Barnacle'. In the 'Gabba Test, 1958, batted 458 minutes to score 68. Was also a fine exponent of swing and seam bowling.

BILL LAWRY: like Bailey had a reputation for slow, deliberate play. Captained Australia, opened the batting and these days is known for his expert, often excited, commentary with the Nine network. Races pigeons, too.

ALAN DAVIDSON: great Australian left-handed all-rounder of the 50s who, apart from being a big-hitting batsman and superb swing bowler, was such a smart close-in fielder team mates called him 'The Claw'. These days he's president of the NSW Cricket Association.

DAVID LLOYD: a gritty little left-hand opening batsman for England when its batsmen had to face up to Lillee and Thomson. Despite suffering plenty of painful knocks retained his quite marvellous sense of humour.

IAN CHAPPELL: just about everyone who played under the tough, uncompromising leadership of 'Chappelli' rates him the best captain. A gutsy batsman and a great first slip fielder. Now a commentator with the Nine Network.

HENRY BLOFELD: was a handy cricketer in his youth but these days is known for his colourful, and unique, commentary on radio and in the media. Sydney's famous Hill crowd paid him the ultimate tribute by naming a stand after him . . . The Henry Blowfly Stand.

DEREK RANDALL: if you can have a saucy cricketer then Randall is the one. Loved to chat with fast bowlers intent only on pinning him with a bouncer, was brilliantly alert in the field and even delighted in performing the odd handstand while patrolling the covers.

JOHN GLEESON: made a late debut for Australia, aged 28, as a wily spinner whose freakish delivery action left the batsman more often than not confused as to which way the ball would turn.

PETER ROEBUCK: plays with Somerset in the England County competition and captained an England XI to Holland, but best known in Australia for his musings on the game in broadsheet newspapers.

ARTHUR MORRIS: legendary left-hand Australian batsman in the postwar era. Engaged in some nerve-wracking battles with the great England bowler Alec Bedser.

KEITH STACKPOLE: short, beefy Australian opening batsman of the Chappell era. Loved to hook and cut the fast bowlers and played with an adventure that had many threatening to tear out their hair—or worse, Stackpole's!

NEIL HAWKE: following a fine career during which he established himself as a smart swing bowler, he very nearly died during a long illness. Recovered to become one of Adelaide's most prominent cricket commentators.

NORMAN O'NEILL: tall, dark and handsome batsman of the 60s whose cover drive and cover fielding made crowds gasp such was their beauty. These days he's a radio commentator with the ABC.

DOUG WALTERS: one of the great characters of cricket. Possessed a rare talent with the bat, a unique ability with the ball and a dry wit which made him one of the game's much-loved sons. Also has a smoke, a drink and a bet.

BOB WILLIS: tall, gangly, thin England fast bowler with a tearaway run-in that only added to the unorthodoxy of his action. Even so it did nothing to reduce his effectiveness, nor his popularity with crowds, who loved his Beatle-like hairstyle.

DENNIS LILLEE: very fast bowler, undoubtedly one of the greatest of all time. Had a lovely flowing, high-stepping run and a pure action. Liked to appeal to umpires by pointing his index fingers skywards . . . a strong hint that the umpire should do likewise!

TONY GREIG: former England captain. An all-rounder whose flair for improvisation allowed him to bat effectively against the Lillee and Thomson menace and to bowl medium fast or offspin. Many recall that neither measure worried David Hookes during the Centenary Test, 1977.

DICKIE BIRD: a famous English umpire who wears one of those longish white coats with the sleeves pushed up, and one of those white cloth caps. Loves to have a chat with the players during the course of play.

BRIAN JOHNSTON: 'Jonners' is a commentator with the BBC in England. He seems to eat lots of cakes sent in by listeners, and even humble pie over on-air gaffes which he acknowledges with a hearty laugh.

IAN REDPATH: a dour batsman from Victoria who mostly opened for Australia with Keith Stackpole during the Chappell era. Now runs a smart antique shop in country Victoria.

GODFREY EVANS: England's wicket-keeper in the 50s, he was fearless about standing on the stumps to fastish bowlers or diving high and wide to gather in wayward returns. These days he sets the bookies' odds on cricket matches in England.

GREG CHAPPELL: the master batsman. Enthralled crowds all over the world with his glorious strokeplay. Will be remembered as one of the most technically correct players Australia has ever produced. A superb fielder, a more than useful bowler and a most astute captain.

IAN WOOLDRIDGE: rated by many as the world's premier sporting columnist, but has a particular affinity with cricket, especially the Ashes battles.

COLIN COWDREY: a classic case of a cricketer whose looks deceived. His portly build belied his agility in the slips and also the grace with which he wielded the bat. One of the game's true gentlemen.

STEVE WAUGH: twin brother of Mark, who has also played for his country. Steve is a classic hitter off the back foot, and, until plagued by a back stress fracture, bowled fast medium with cunning and guile.

ALLAN LAMB: the only slaughter around when this chunky little batsman is at the crease is slaughter of the bowling. One of England's premier batsmen who has been rewarded with the vice-captaincy.

GRAHAM GOOCH: England's latest captain who stunned the West Indies recently by taking a Test off them, then had his hand broken for his trouble. Also an effective opening batsman and slip field.

MARK TAYLOR: a solid opening batsman in every sense of the word. He has stormed the Test match scene with a rash of highly concentrated centuries against England, Sri Lanka and Pakistan. Found time in between to score a couple for NSW, too.

DEAN JONES: fleet-of-foot and just loves to prove it when the spinners are on, or he's chasing a ball towards the boundary. Arguably world cricket's greatest limited-overs batsman of the moment. Strong Test record, too.

TERRY ALDERMAN: observers nicknamed him 'The Smiling Assassin' during the 1989 Ashes tour to England because of all the photos that showed him bowling with a grin of anticipation fixed to sun-creamed lips, as he sought yet another England leg before victim.

RODNEY MARSH: his magnificent career spanned more than a decade. In the beginning they dubbed him 'Iron Gloves'. By the time he'd finished, he was 'Golden Gloves'. One of the scallywags of cricket who wrote himself into the record books by capturing a world-record number of victims.

SIMON O'DONNELL: has fought back from a life-threatening health crisis to take his place among the top 20 cricketers in Australia. He is especially effective in the limited-overs style game. Loves confusing batsmen with his slower ball.